The Vegan Guide *To* New York City

Rynn Berry & Chris A. Suzuki

With Barry Litsky, J.D.

Published by

Ethical | Living

This book is dedicated to FM Esfandiary, Napoleao Nelson Salgado-Santos, and to all people who respect animals enough not to eat them or consume their byproducts.

•

Copyright © 2007 by Rynn Berry, and Chris Abreu-Suzuki.

All rights reserved under International and Pan American Copyright Conventions. No part of the publication may be reproduced, stored in a retrieval system, or transmitted, in any form or by any means electronic, mechanical, photocopying, recording, or otherwise, without the prior written permission of the publisher. Brief quotations permitted for review purposes.

Thirteenth edition, 2007

ISBN 13: 978-0-9788132-0-8
ISBN 10: 0-9788132-0-0

Library of Congress Number 2001-135857

This book is printed on durable, acid-free paper.

Published in the United States by Ethical Living
P O Box 8174
JAF Station
New York, NY 10116

Cover design and title page design by Donna Hughes and Dr. Chris Abreu-Suzuki. Cover drawing by Sarah Caplan.

Our thanks to Diane Brandt, Enrique Martinez, and J.C. Oliveira.

CONTENTS

A Word from the Authors	5
A Few Notes on Dining in New York	6
The Restaurants	8
Harlem	8
Upper West Side	11
Upper East Side	13
Midtown West (and Chelsea)	16
Midtown East (and Gramercy Park)	22
Greenwich Village	30
East Village	36
SoHo	46
Below Canal Street (Chinatown, Tribeca, Financial District)	51
Brooklyn	54
Queens	62
Top Ten Juice Bars	67
Food Shopping Tips	70
Favorite Shops	71
Greenmarkets (Farmer's markets)	78
Rawfood Resources	82
Bookstores	85
Glossary	86
Cruelty-Free Shoes	88
Mail Order	89

Why Veganism?	90
For More Information	91
Map of Top 22 Favorite Restaurants	ultimate page

Appreciations

"More than a food guide, a portable conscience. "

                New York Times

"The Vegan Guide to New York City is a very complete Guide!"

                The New York Daily News

"Packed with information and insightful commentary, THE VEGAN GUIDE TO NEW YORK CITY invites you to take a juicy, cholesterol-free, cruelty-free bite out of the Big Apple.

                Michael Klaper, M.D.
                Author, *Vegan Nutrition: Pure and Simple*

"Indispensable for the traveling vegan, this guide will most definitely enhance the vegan experience in New York. As a long-time resident of this city, I learned a great deal!"

                Gary Francione, Professor of Law, Rutgers University
                Director, Animal Rights Law Clinic

A WORD FROM THE AUTHORS

We love food. Whatever image the uninformed may hold of vegans as joyless ascetics who subsist on carrots and brown rice, it certainly does not hold true for us. We love to eat from a world of varied cuisines—a simple macrobiotic meal of miso soup and steamed vegetables one day, a sumptuous Italian feast of grilled pizza with roasted sweet peppers and portobello mushrooms the next, a rich Thai or Indian curry dinner the third—and one of the joys of New York City is that you can find them all within the same block. That's because New York is a world city.

The Vegan Guide to New York City was launched back in 1994, when Rynn Berry, Max Friedman, and Dan Mills, under the tutelage of Alex Bourke, author of *Vegetarian London,* put together the first slender edition. That same year Dan went back to London to practice law, and Max went to graduate school to get a Ph.D. in American History. That left Rynn Berry in New York City to carry on with the Vegan Guide. In the years since, Rynn has put out a new edition of the guide annually. In 2001, he joined forces with Chris Abreu Suzuki, and Barry Litsky to put out the first quality paperback edition of the Vegan Guide. Rynn, Chris and Barry met at the Farm Sanctuary, a refuge for farm animals in Watkins Glen, New York.

Rynn Berry is the historical advisor to the North American Vegetarian Society. He is the author of several seminal books on vegetarianism; they include *The New Vegetarians, Famous Vegetarians and Their Favorite Recipes, Hitler: Neither Vegetarian Nor Animal Lover,* and *Food for The Gods Vegetarianism and the World's Religions.* In 2004, Rynn was commissioned to write a 6,000 word entry on the history of vegetarianism in the US for the Oxford Encyclopedia of Food and Drink in America. Rynn contributes frequently to both scholarly and spiritual publications.

Chris Abreu-Suzuki, Ph.D., is a professor of Mathematics, a long distance runner, who has won many races, a fervent animal rights activist and a connoisseur of vegan food. She's been a vegan since 1992 and an ethical vegetarian since 1977.

Barry Litsky, an intellectual property lawyer, who lives in New York City, does *pro bono* work for animal rights causes. He is also a vegetarian gourmet, who loves to whip up vegan meals for friends in his apartment.

A FEW NOTES ON DINING IN NEW YORK...

There are more than 100 restaurants described in this book, but by no means should you limit yourself to them. New York is a city where you have the wide world at your doorstep, and you should not hesitate to plunge right in. All the restaurants listed in this guide offer vegan meals, but vegans will also do well at restaurants that do not go out of their way to cater to them, bearing in mind a few basic principles.

There are two centers for **Indian food** in town. One is 6th Street between 1st and 2nd Avenues, a block known as "Little India" for its cheek-by-jowl Indian restaurants. The joke is that there's one kitchen and a conveyor belt. Less well-known to tourists is the community on Lexington around 28th Street, where the patrons are often Indian, too. As a rule, you should ask if they cook with *ghee* (clarified butter). We've listed Indian restaurants that use oil in most of their dishes, but ask anyway. You can request that they leave off the *raita* (yogurt with cucumbers).

There has been a boom in the popularity of **Mexican food** in the United States in the past few years, notably when salsa bypassed ketchup in condiment sales. In Mexico, Mexican food is based on corn or wheat with beans, but prepared with lard, cheese and meat stock, making strict vegan travel there a challenge. In New York City, there are a few authentic and many cheap Americanized places to eat Mexican food unsuitable for vegans. However, the last five years has seen an explosion in the number of trendy, "Cal-Mex" or "Tex-Mex" or "San Francisco Style" restaurants serving a healthy variation of Mexican cuisine prepared without lard, containing fresh vegetables and usually with the option of soy cheese, whole wheat tortillas and brown rice. (Almost all soy cheeses contain casein, a milk derivative; most tofu sour cream does not. See Glossary.) We have included addresses for these chains of healthy, vegan-friendly Mexican restaurants, where some of the best meals in the city are to be had. While they are similar, we give Burritoville a slight edge over the others:

Some of the most talented chefs in town are at moderate to expensive **Italian** restaurants. Vegans can always find something to eat here, if you request that your food be prepared with olive oil instead of butter, and make sure they leave out the common flavorings of Parmesan cheese and prosciutto (ham). Fresh pasta is often, but not always, made with egg. At **Thai** restaurants, it's dried shrimp and fish sauce you want to look out for. But we should offer this caveat: Since non-veg restaurants use utensils and working surfaces that may have come in contact with animal flesh, it is always preferable to eat in vegetarian/ vegan restaurants to avoid cross-contamination. Now go ahead and explore.

Nearly every restaurant in this guide offers **take-out** (meals to take home) and almost all of them also will deliver food right to your door, if you're in the area (say, within fifteen to twenty blocks). Because this service is nearly universal, we have specified only when a restaurant does NOT deliver or serve take-out. Otherwise, if the weather's bad or you'd rather stay indoors, you can call any one of these places and have your dinner in the comfort of your own room. Delivery is almost always free, usually with a minimum total order of $7-12, and you should tip your delivery person 15% of the bill. You can simply call up and tell them what you want, or ask what they have without meat or milk products; or, better still, do as New Yorkers do and start your own collection of take-out menus from your favorite restaurants .

Most **health food shops** offer an assortment of ready-to-eat foods for vegans—hummus sandwiches, nutburgers and salads—in the refrigerator case. These tend to be OK, range in price from two to four dollars and can be just the thing if you want a quick snack. We've made a note by health food shops that go a little further, with a fresh salad bar, sandwich counter or buffet.

More and more liquor stores in New York stock **organic wines**, and of these, several labels are vegan—they use no fish or eggs in the "fining" (clarifying) process. Look for anything by the Organic Wine Works label or anything by Frey except the 1991 Cabernet, which was fined with egg whites. If you can't find them anywhere, try Warehouse Wines and Spirits at 735 Broadway (at Astor Place) or the slightly more expensive Astor Wines and Spirits at Lafayette and Astor.

An important note for our foreign readers: **tax and tip** are NOT included in the price at American restaurants, so figure on adding another 8.65% for the city and 15-20% for the service. American servers get paid an abysmal hourly wage and earn most of their salary from tips, so this is not really optional: unless you get terrible service, everyone leaves 15% as a matter of routine, and it's nicer to leave 20%. An exception is when there is no server, as in buffets or self-serve cafeterias; and when you dine in a group of more than five persons, the tip ("gratuity") may be figured into your total. People who deliver take-out to your door should also get a 15% tip.

A valid current **Student I.D.** will get you 10-15% off at many restaurants and some shops. The restaurants are grouped by neighborhood, and listed alphabetically within each neighborhood.

A NOTE ON OUR POLICY OF RESTAURANT SELECTION:

In 1994, when we first launched this guide, the number of vegan and vegetarian restaurants were rather sparse; so we included some vegetarian friendly restaurants that served some meat, but went out of their way to accommodate vegetarians. As of 1996, it was our feeling that we should no longer include any restaurants that served animal flesh of any kind--be it fish or fowl, snail or cow--because all restaurants have become friendlier to vegetarians; so to continue to feature vegetarian friendly restaurants in the Guide would make it meaningless. The vegetarian friendly restaurants that were included in the original guide were grandfathered in and phased out as they closed. In a few instances, restaurants started out as being vegan, then started serving increasing amounts of meat. These were so egregiously non-veg. that we had to delete them from the guide. But from then on, only vegetarian and vegan restaurants were to be included. That's why you may not find the trendy almost-vegetarian restaurant that you've been hearing about. Look to the conventional guides for those. Furthermore, in rating and ranking restaurants, we add and subtract points depending on how vegan they are. In other words, if they use honey or dairy products in their dishes, they will be penalized for it.

The Madras Cafe
Indian Vegetarian

'Madras specializes in the vegetarian cuisine of southern India, pungent, vividly spiced food that can make carnivores forget they're not eating meat.'
'It's the food that shines, and this food travels well.' **The New York Times**

Strictly Kosher: Supervised by Rabbi Pacec Ackerman

Catering for All Occassions
We specialize in South Indian, Vegan Friendly & North Indian Cuisine

Phone: 212-254-8002
Fax: 212-684-2788
www.madrascafenyc.com
79 Second Avenue, New York, NY 10003

Tiengarden
Vegan Restaurant

Tel: 212-388-1364

170 Allen Street, NYC 10002
(1 & ½ blocks south of E. Houston)
Hours: 12 noon - 10 pm
(Closed on Sunday)

Lan Cafe

342 East 6th Street, New York
(212) 228-8325
Open Sunday-Thursday 12-10PM
Friday & Saturday 12PM-12AM

Visit FARM SANCTUARY

Tour our farm that is home to hundreds of rescued pigs, goats, turkeys, cows, and other farm animals.

Call Today!

22-06

Tour admission buy one, get one free with this coupon.
Open May - October   Call 607-583-2225 for tour schedule
www.FarmSanctuary.org

Come Back to Where It All Began!

Integral Yoga®
Natural Apothecary

The Highest-Quality
Vegetarian Supplements,
Herbal Extracts,
and Formulas
234 West 13th Street
212-645-3051

Integral Yoga®
Natural Foods

Organic Products
Based on the Principles of
Purity, Nonviolence, and
Balanced Living
229 West 13th Street
212-243-2642

THE RESTAURANTS

ve=vegan
v=fleshless with vegan options
AE=American Express
MC=Mastercard
V=Visa
D=Discover

Full service means waiters take your order and bring your food. Counter service means you order at the counter and carry your meal to your table (these are usually cheaper, more casual places, often with paper plates). Prices listed are for typical vegan entrees.
Address is listed opposite restaurant name.
Nearest cross-streets are under address for easy location.

 Indicates we especially recommend this restaurant for the quality of the food.

HARLEM
(North of Central Park)

RAW SOUL [ve]
Counter service
Organic juice bar & deli
$4-15 (no cards)
No alcohol
www.rawsoul@rawsoul.com

348 West 145th Street
bet. St. Nicholas/ Edgecomb Avenues
212-491-4263
M-Sa 9am-9pm
Su 11am-4pm

This is the real soul food--not the ham hocks and fat backs that the plantation owners forced on the slaves. The real soul food was the living- foods diet of fruits and vegetables that the African peoples lived on before so many of them were transported in chains to the New World. Eddie and Lillian Robinson, husband and wife partners, have helped to revive the tradition of eating healthy and delicious unfired foods in the black community. Theirs is some of the tastiest and most affordable living food in town.

By profession, this talented duo are tap dancers; Lillian is also a jazz singer with a CD to her credit. All their artistic talent, and, as they like to emphasize, "love" go into the making of their mouthwatering living vegan food. Vegan is the operative word here. Eddie and Lillian stress that they go out of their way to avoid using dairy products. They serve their home-made almond and sesame milks instead; and they use dates, and agave (cactus) nectar in lieu of honey.

When we arrived, Lillian and Eddie regaled us with a raw Curried Almond-Zucchini Soup that was out of this world. Then they served us a raw Middle Eastern plate consisting of raw Hummus, Tabbouleh and living Falafel Balls made from fava beans. For dessert, Eddie served us a scrumptious living Pear Tart made with macadamia nuts, walnuts, almonds, cashew-cream sauce, and Turkish figs. Need we say m-m-m-m-m-m?

As we were leaving, we remembered that we were planning a picnic on the morrow; so we took home with us a couple of Egyptian Wraps, which consisted of a marinated mixture of zucchini, eggplant, yellow squash and vidalia onions, wrapped in a collard green leaf. We also took along a few bottles each of their live home-made Sorrel Punch, containing hibiscus, wheat berries, dates, raisins, star anise and lime, and their home-made living Ginger Beer, containing rejuvelac, dates, raisins, ginger, cinnamon, and lime.

• In 2006, Ras Dawitt, the chef-owner of the popular, but short-lived raw vegan juice bar, Earthly Juices, joined the staff at Raw Soul. At about the same time, Raw Soul moved around the corner into larger quarters to accommodate their growing clientele. Their new space is at street level. Inside, the walls are hung with paintings by local African-American artists on loan from the nearby Simmons gallery. Amidst these vibrant paintings, and the warm ambiance, you may sip the juices and smoothies from the juice bar and savor dishes from the raw deli such as the Rasta Pasta, the Barbecue Burger, The Collard Wrap the Personal Pizza and The Tamale Pie. Eating lustily of these left us deeply satisfied, but still craving more. The desserts run the gamut from raw cakes, cheesecakes, and pies to an array of ice-creams. All their menu items have such robust flavors that you'll probably want to learn how to duplicate them at home. If so, Lillian offers instruction in a series of hands-on courses.

STRICTLY ROOTS [ve]

Counter service
West Indian
$5-10 (no cards)
No alcohol

2058 Adam Clayton Powell Blvd.
at 123rd Street
212-864-8699
M-Sa 12pm-11pm
Su 12pm-10pm

As the Rasta chef says, there is nothing served here that "crawls, walks, swims or flies." The menu changes every day and consists of items like broccoli & tofu, chick pea stew, seitan, falafel, tofu tempura, or veggie duck. The daily staples include millet, brown rice, greens and fried plantains. You can order small, medium or large portions of any combination of the above for $5, $7.50 and $10 respectively. Don't expect gourmet presentation, but it's good, wholesome stuff. They also have a variety of smaller dishes (e.g. veggie burger, vegetable salad) and beverages—juices, soy milk, and non-alcoholic ginger beer.

UPTOWN JUICE BAR[ve]

Counter service
West Indian
$6-8.50 (no cards)
No alcohol

54 West 125th Street
bet. 5th & Lenox
212-289-9501
daily 8am-10pm

A cross between a small cafe and a juice bar, Uptown Juice Bar is to be prized as much for its food as for its juices. Along with an array of juice combinations and smoothies, it serves delicious Caribbean-style vegan food. And although the menu contains alarming words like beef and fish, these are to be understood as "mock beef" and "mock fish." For instance there is a "turkey" salad, a "chicken" salad and a "fish" salad, but no turkey, chicken or fish died to produce these dishes. They're entirely ersatz and are very tasty. We had one of their combination meals that consisted of collard greens, tofu with black mushrooms, and a vegan shepherd's pie. To wash down this delectable grub, have one of their fruit smoothies or a juice tonic that is designed to cure whatever ails you. For impotence, drink a potent brew of carrot, parsley, cucumber, orange, and papaya juices. For asthma, gulp down a beverage containing carrot, celery, and grapefruit juice. Of course, if you're a vegan of long-standing, you probably don't have any of these ailments, so toast your good health--and your good fortune in being a vegan--with a fruit smoothie instead.

 Indicates we especially recommend this restaurant for the quality of the food.

UPPER WEST SIDE
(West 59th Street and Above)

AYURVEDA CAFE [v]
Full service
South Indian
Prix-fixe $5.95(lunch)-9.95(dinner) (all cards)
No alcohol

706 Amsterdam Avenue
at 94th Street
212-932-2400
daily 11:30am-11:30pm

With its mango-hued walls and mottled sky blue ceilings, the Ayurveda Cafe resembles nothing so much as a film set for an early Merchant-Ivory movie, like Shakespeare Wallah or Bombay Talkie. So, it's not surprising to learn that the owner, Tirlok Malik, is a film director, who has parlayed a side interest in Indian cuisine into what seems to my taste buds to be one of the best Indian restaurants in town. Part Ismail Merchant, part Deepak Chopra with the Chopra ascendant, Malik has based his restaurant's dishes on the teachings of one of the four sacred books of Vedic Hinduism, which dates back at least 3,000 years--the *Ayurveda* (which means "knowledge of life" in Sanskrit.) Essentially, Ayurvedic cuisine tries to combine the six tastes, sweet. sour, salty, astringent, bitter and pungent, in order to produce a cuisine that is properly balanced for your body type. It certainly was right for my olfactory type. The Thali that I tasted was lightly spiced and lightly cooked so that you could taste each vegetable. I had to skip the raitas and desserts because they all contained dairy products and /or honey. Otherwise, a vegan can dine very handsomely here.

CAFE VIVA [A.K.A. **VIVA HERBAL PIZZERIA**]

Counter service
Italian vegetarian, kosher
$1.52-7.95 (all cards)
No alcohol

2578 Broadway
bet.97th//98th Streets
212-663-8482
daily 11am-11pm

The founder, Tony Iracani, tells us that Cafe Viva is the only Italian vegetarian restaurant in the US, which after sampling the vegetarian antipasto and the tasty cheeseless pizzas, strikes us as shameful. Italian restaurateurs should beat a path to Cafe Viva to see how vegan Italian food is done, then go forth and do likewise. We had the Pizza Pura, a dairy-free, yeast-free spelt crust, topped with tofu marinated in Miso, grilled veggies and spinach with a vegetarian antipasto on the side. The fridge is stocked with healthful sodas such as Twisted Bean Vanilla Brew, Borealis Birch Beer, Ginseng tonics and China Cola. Recently Cafe Viva has expanded its menu to include a super anti-oxidant pizza; a Zen pizza, which features a green-tea herbal crust; tofu marinated with herbs, and a green tea pesto; it is topped off with a layer of maitake and shitake mushrooms. Another favorite is the Santa Rosa, which consists of a whole wheat crust layered with tofu marinated in miso, and topped off with sun-dried tomatoes and roasted garlic. Viva offers two types of vegan Lasagna as well as vegan Calzones made from spelt and whole wheat. Other pastas such as Raviolis, Strombolis, and Zitis are made from scratch and can be veganized to order. The service staff is friendly and helpful to the point of being obsequious. One of the great pleasures apart from the food is that one can sit and read a paper or chat with a companion for hours without being hurried or pressured. We say, "Viva! Cafe Viva!"

DALE & THOMAS POPCORN [v]

Counter-service
Indiana popcorn
$3.95-5.95 (all major cards)
No alcohol

2170 Broadway
at 76th Street
212-769-0150
M-Sa 11am-11pm
Su 11am-12am

This is one of those single-food-item eateries--like Hummus Place, Pommes Frites, Cafe Viva Pizzeria, Moshe's Falafel and the Dosa Hut--in which New York abounds. If one can make a meal of Pommes Frites, then why not dine on popcorn that is freshly popped on the spot? Select from an array of flavors-- Back-Yard Barbecue, Drive-In, Kettle Corn, Caramel, Chocolate Chunk On Caramel, Dark and White Chocolate, etc. If you're a vegan, you'll want to eschew the Cheddar and the Chocolate, which are made with cheese and milk-powder respectively, but the others are blessedly dairy-free.[Canola oil is used instead of butter]. Munch them on the spot, smuggle them into your favorite Bijou, or take them home and snack on them while watching the Purple Rose of Cairo on your DVD player.

See other location under Midtown East

UPPER EAST SIDE
(East 59th Street and Above)

BLUE GREEN [ve]

Counter service
Organic raw food cafe/ juice bar
$7.95-14.95 (all cards)
No alcohol.
www.bluegreenjuice.com

203 East 74th Street
bet. Second/ Third Avenues
212-744-1460
daily 9am-8pm

Compact and self-contained, like a space capsule, Blue Green is primarily a juice bar, where some of the most delicious organic juice combinations and smoothies are served up. (Our favorite--the No.11(cacao, black cherry, banana and coconut water). Blue Green is also one of chef Matthew Kenney's satellite rawfood cafes of which the Plant in Dumbo is, as it were, "the mother planet." At planet Plant, celestial rawfood eats are crafted under Kenney's supervision; then the unfired eats are shipped to each of the Blue Green Cafes. Spicy Mango Spring Roll (crispy vegetables, young coconut, green papaya, and fresh herbs), and The Torta, (which is like a squash lasagna), were our favorites, but we also enjoyed improvising our own unfired entree by purchasing a container of raw flaxseed crackers and dipping them in a Mango Salsa. We followed this with a delectable raw cheesecake, and we indulged our inner Little Jack Horner by spooning up the plump cherries at the bottom of the Black Forest Pudding.

See other locations in Soho and Brooklyn

CANDLE CAFE [ve]

Full service
Vegan, organic
$6--18 (all cards)
Organic wine and beer
www. candlecafe.com

1307 Third Avenue
bet. 74th/75th Streets
212-472-0970 & 472-7169(fax)
M-Sa 11:30am-10:30pm
Su 11:30am-9:30pm

Back in the days when Bart Potenza, Candle's tousle-haired founder, ran a juice bar called the Healthy Candle, he dreamed of owning a vegan restaurant. A few years later, he realized his dream when he opened Candle Cafe. Twelve years on, Candle Cafe has metamorphosed into one of New York's most popular eateries where celebrity watchers can spot environmental- and health-conscious actors like Woody Harrelson, and Alicia Silverstone, or prominent Animal Rights activists like Eddy Lama of *The Witness* , or Harold Brown of *The Peaceable Kingdom.*

They come here because Bart and his partner, Joy Pierson, have a history of supporting environmental and animal rights causes and because they serve up some of the tastiest vegan food in town. We found just about everything on the menu appetizing, but our particular favorites were as follows: Our favorite appetizer was the Seitan Chimichurri (South American marinated seitan skewers with creamy citrus herb dressing). Our favorite entree was the Cabernet-Infused Seitan (pan-seared cajun seitan served with steamed greens and coleslaw). We also relished the Tuscan Lasagna with Grilled Summer Vegetables, Tofu-Basil Ricotta, and Seitan Ragout with a Truffled Tomato Sauce. For dessert, we fell upon the Chocolate Mousse Pie and the Decadent Chocolate Cake with Vanilla Frosting.

When it comes to Seitan dishes, which are the forte of both Candle Cafe and Candle 79, no other restaurant can hold a candle to the Candle.

CANDLE 79 [ve]

Full service
Global organic vegan
$7–24 (all cards)
Organic wines, beers and sakes.

154 East 79th Street
at Lexington Avenue
212-537-7179
M-Sa Lunch, 12pn-3:30pm
    Dinner, 5:30pm-10:30pm
Su   Brunch, 12pm-4pm
    Dinner, 5-10pm

Now at last New York's Upper East Side has a posh vegan restaurant serving Global Organic style vegan cuisine that can rival --in elegance as well as in sapidity--the Millennium in San Francisco, Chu Chai in Montreal, Vegethus in Sao Paulo, Bann's Vegetarian Cafe in Edinburgh and Hangawi in midtown New York.

Bart Potenza and his partner Joy Pierson have transformed an unprepossessing two-story town house that was formerly a prosaic restaurant called the Dining Room into a restaurant whose interior design is as ravishing as are the dishes on its bill of fare.

Start with the Teaser: Live Heirloom Tomato Tartare. Then proceed to the Wild Mushroom Salad with Arugala, Grape Tomatoes, Roasted Cippolini Onions, and Creamy Horseradish Dressing. Then on to the maincourse of Cashew Crusted Tofu with Brown Rice Arame Pilaf, Ginger-Sautéed Asian Greens, Grilled Shitkakes and a Miso-Sake Sauce, or try The Pumpkin Seed Crusted Tempeh with Tomatilla Sauce and Sweet Corn. If you're a rawfoodist have the Live Zucchini Lasagna with Cashew Ricotta, Wild Mushrooms, Herb Pesto, and Fresh Tomato Ragout. Finish with their Mexican Chocolate Cake, which is so sinful that it could only have come from south of the border.

Be sure to check the current menu on-line (www. candlecafe.com), as it changes with the season according to local organic produce. A special gluten-free menu is available. Private party rooms are also available.

Much of the credit for Candle 79's dazzling menu is owing to head chef Angel Ramos, and pastry chef Jorge Pineda. We are avid fans of their seitan dishes both at Candle Cafe and at Candle 79. They have raised the preparation of Seitan to high art. Indeed, their Seitan Picatta with Creamed Spinach with Roasted Garlic Mashed Potatoes, and Lemon-Caper Sauce should make Seitan worshippers of even the most fundamentalist carnivore. Congratulations to Candle 79 for being named "New York Naturally's Restaurant of the Year for 2006!

GOBO [ve]

Full service
Organic, Asian-Western fusion cuisine
$8.00-15.00 (all cards)
Organic beer & wine
www.goborestaurant.com

1426 Third Avenue
at 81st Street
212-288-4686
Su-We 11:30am-11:30pm
Th-Sa 11:30am-12am

See the description under East Village.

PONGAL[v]

Full service
Indian vegetarian
$6.95-9.95 (major cards)
No alcohol

1154 First Avnue
at 63rd Street
212-355-4600
Th 11:30am-10pm
F-Su 11:30am-10:30pm

See the description under Midtown East.

NEW!

East West Books & Cafe

VEGETARIAN BISTRO

Organic, Natural
Vegan, Raw
Coffee, Tea, Chai
Snacks & Meals
Free Wi-Fi
Catering & Events
Zen Inspired Décor

78 Fifth Avenue bet 13th & 14th
Open 7 Days / 10 am – 9 pm
Café 212.243.3667
Bookstore 212.243.5994

www.eastwestnyc.com

MIDTOWN WEST and Chelsea
(West 14th to West 59th Streets)

BLOSSOM[ve]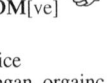

Full Service
Global vegan, orgainc
$4.00-6.00 (all cards)
Orgainc beer & wine
www.blossomnyc.com

187 Ninth Avenue
bet. 21st/ 22nd Streets
212-627-1144
daily 11:30am-10:30pm

Erstwhile actors, Ronen Seri, and his wife Pamela, couldn't find a restaurant to satisfy their recherché vegan tastes; so they decided to open their own place. We vegan foodies are all in their debt. For now we have someplace to go besides Candle '79, on the upper east side, and Millennium, in San Francisco, to slake our appetite for organic vegan haute cuisine.
    Indeed the restaurant's interior has a touch of the theater about it. With its chic town-house setting; its cozy fireplace; its burnished wood tables; its floor-to-ceiling draperies; it looks like the perfect stage set for a posh restaurant
    Despite their restaurant's high-toned elegance, Ronen and Pamela are not above stating, right on their menu, that "Blossom is first and foremost animal caring." Consequently, their "food is not only organic, it is also dairy and cholesterol free." This is the first time we know of that a restaurateur has had the courage to remind his/her patrons that conventional non-veg. food involves the wanton sacrifice of our fellow creatures.
    We would eat at Blossom out of solidarity with Ronen and Pamela--just to pay tribute to their ethical approach to food preparation--but, fortunately, their food is so extraordinary that we also eat there for the sheer yumminess of the dishes.
    Everyone we know. in our circle of vegan friends, raves about Blossom's appetizers--especially the South Asian Lumpia (curried seitan and potatoes wrapped in a crispy chickpea crepe, served with mango onion sambal). And, we are here to confirm that it, and the Black-Eyed Pea Cake (crispy cake of yukon gold potato & black-eyed peas, served with chipotle aioli) are as fresh and peppery as they're cracked up to be.
    We're confessed seitan worshippers; so we reveled in the Barbecued Seitan Sandwich (barbecued seitan and caramelized onions with fresh cut fries or salad); and the Seitan Medallions (pan seared seitan cutlets served with herbed soft polenta and broccoli rabe). They would have delighted Old Split-foot himself, [who like most ungulates is doubtless a vegan].
    For dessert we had the Chocolate Ganache Cake (a layered combination of rich chocolate ganache and chocolate cake). And the Pineapple Crepe (grilled pineapple wrapped in a crepe served with coconut reduction and green tea or vanilla ice-cream). It was a fitting climax to this play in three courses. We were chagrined--as with most extraordinary theater--only that it had to end.

DALE & THOMAS POPCORN [v]

Counter-service
Indiana popcorn
$3.95-5.95 (all major cards)
No alcohol

1592 Broadway
at 48th Street
212-581-1872
M-Sa 11am-11pm
Su 11am-12am

This is one of those single-food-item eateries--like Hummus Place, Pommes Frites, Cafe Viva Pizzeria, Moshe's Falafel and the Dosa Hut--in which New York abounds. If one can make a meal of Pommes Frites, then why not dine on popcorn that is freshly popped on the spot? Select from an array of flavors-- Back-Yard Barbecue, Drive-In, Kettle Corn, Caramel, Chocolate Chunk On Caramel, Dark and White Chocolate, etc. If you're a vegan, you'll want to eschew the Cheddar and the Chocolate, which are made with cheese and milk-powder respectively, but the others are blessedly dairy-free.[Canola oil is used instead of butter].Munch them on the spot, smuggle them into your favorite Bijou, or take them home and snack on them while watching the Purple Rose of Cairo on your DVD player.

See other location under Upper West Side.

DIMPLE [v]

Self-service
Indian, kosher
$3.95-8.95 (all major cards)
No alcohol

11 West 30th Street
bet. Fifth Avenue/Broadway
212-643-9464
M-F 8:30am-10pm
Sa, Su 11am-10pm

This fast-food Indian vegetarian restaurant will put dimples in the cheeks of famished midtown office workers who at lunch time are hard put to find a good vegetarian restaurant in the vicinity. Not only is the food good here, but it's so economical as to make the budget-conscious vegetarian consider eating here rather than brown-bagging it. The cost of a take-out Thali that includes a choice of three vegetables, dal or kadhi, rice, 2 roti or one naan, or 2 pakoras, raita, pickle, salad and a sweet is only $5.99. Each day they offer a different Thali from a different region of India: Monday it's a Gujarati Thali; Thursday, it's a Sindhi Thali. The only caveat is that vegans must be careful to ask which dishes contain dairy products and which do not.

See other location in Queens.

FRUIT SALADS, FRUIT SHAKES[ve]

Food cart
Fruit salads and shakes
$3.00-6.00 (no cards)
No alcohol

Corner 46th Street
at Sixth Avenue
(no phone)
M-F 7am-4pm

Just as we had opined in our review of Govinda's--that one of New York's finest vegan restaurants is actually a food cart--so we must assert that one of New York's best rawfood restaurants and juice bars is really a food cart. The cart is owned by a jaunty middle-aged Vietnamese couple named Vo and Do An. Their fruit salads and shakes are ambrosial. The salads, which range in price from $2.50-$3.50, can be made to order in any combination of fruits and vegetables such as mango, pears, lettuce and carrots. There is a wide array of fruits to choose from--papayas, cherries, blueberries, strawberries, cantaloupes, etc.

The shakes, which range in price from $3.00 for a small to $4.00 for a large, are so generous as to be a meal in themselves. Choose from such combinations as mango, banana and pineapple, and strawberry, mango and banana. There are ten possible combinations to select from.

The word "shake" has the connotation in North America of a beverage that combines fruit, ice-cream and milk, but no dairy products are used here. Vo and Do An are from a Buddhist country in which dairy products have traditionally been eschewed on moral grounds. [Eating dairy products like meat-eating is a violation of the first precept of Buddhism, *ahimsa:* "Non-violence to all living creatures."] Consequently, Do An and Vo do not put milk or yogurt in the fruit shakes. or salads. The shakes and salads are composed purely of fruit. Nor do any of their shakes or salads contain frozen fruit or fruit syrups made from concentrate, as do those of most of the juice bars in the city.

Do An and Vo work year round, sleet or snow, rain or shine. But when one drinks their shakes, or eats one of their fruit salads, it always feels like a sun-splashed day in midsummer!

MOSHE'S FALAFEL[ve]

Food cart
Middle Eastern (Israeli), kosher
$4.00-6.00 (no cards)
No alcohol

Corner 46th Street
at Sixth Avenue
(no phone)
M-Th 11am-5pm
F 11am-3pm

Let's face it: most falafel places in the city are just plain "foul-awful!" Mainly, we think, this is because of the cross-contamination. All-too-often, the "foul-awfuls" in non-veg. places are deep-fried in the same rancid oil that is used to cook animal flesh. At this outdoor food cart, however-- because the food is vegan and kosher--none of these concerns apply.

Perhaps it was psychological, but knowing that the falafels weren't contaminated made them taste that much better. Evidently, Moshe's customers concur, because when we sampled his food, there was a line around the block! Portions are generous. Topped with colossal pickles, stuffed with chunks of tomato, fistfuls of lettuce, and drenched with the obligatory tahini sauce, Moshe's Falafels are fully twice the size of the standard-issue falafel sandwich. For those who like their falafels hot, ask for a devilishly piquant hot sauce on the side. Or if you're traveling any distance before eating it, ask for the tahini sauce on the side too. [The trick to eating a falalel sandwich is to eat it on the spot lest the tahini sauce seep into the bread and make it soggy. And nothing tastes worse than a soggy falafel sandwich!] Moshe serves up an ample salad and a selection of vegan soups as well.

NATURAL GOURMET COOKERY SCHOOL [ve]

Full service
Gourmet vegan
$32.00 prix-fixe (all cards)
BYOB

48 West 21st Street
bet 5th and 6th Avenues
212-645-5170
F 6:30pm

Every Friday, the Natural Gourmet Cookery School has a feast that is prepared by the students at the school. The public is invited to partake of the students' cooking, which is vegan. Students, attired as waiters, serve four-course meals at large communal dining tables that are reminiscent of a college refectory. As in a college dining hall, the communal tables encourage the dinner guests to strike up conversations with total strangers, which adds to the convivial atmosphere.

The price for the four-course meal, at thirty-two dollars, is high, but then the cooking rivals that of any four-star restaurant. Truth to tell, we did overhear a few diners grumble about the meagerness of the portions. But the *nouvelle cuisine vegeterienne* style of cookery that is taught here dictates that portions be small. And the very fact that customers cry for more shows that the food is exceptionally tasty.

With the exception of only one item on the menu, we relished the food unreservedly. This was the Crispy Scallion Pancakes that were so crispy they tasted like hockey pucks. But the entree--Savory Baked Tofu Arame Stir-Fry with a Melange of Mushrooms and Fresh Vegetables in a Sweet and Spicy Sauce Served on a Bed of Lettuce and Crispy Rice Noodles--was divine. And the dessert! The dessert! Five Spiced Roasted Peach Pie with vegan Basil Ice-Cream and Sour Cherry Sauce, was sublime.

While everyone was clamoring for seconds and thirds on the vegan Basil Ice-Cream, the door to the kitchen suddenly swung open, and we saw something that we were not supposed to see. We spied the dessert chef downing a soup bowl filled with gobs of vegan Basil Ice-Cream. That's how good it was!

SULLIVAN STREET BAKERY (PIZZERIA) [v]
UPTOWN

Counter service
Pizzas/baked goods
Pizzas $3.00-4.00 (all cards)
No alcohol

533 West 47th Street
bet 10th/ 11th Avenues
212-265-5580
daily 7am-7pm

For lacto-vegetarians who want to go vegan, often the hardest food to give up is Pizza made with cheese. Now at last there is a place that serves vegan pizzas that are every bit as tasty as their non-vegan counterparts. One of them in particular, the Pizza Patate, is so good that Martha Stewart features a recipe for it on her web site. The owner of this bakery-cum-pizzeria, Jim Lahey, actually demonstrated how to make it on Martha's TV show. It's a flat pizza topped with a layer of thinly sliced potatoes. That's how pizzas are done at Sullivan Street. Straightforward and delicious with savory toppings like the sliced Crimini mushrooms of the Pizza Funghi. Or the rosemary, olive oil and salt of the Pizza Bianca. Or the cherry tomatoes and basil of the Pizza Pugliesi. Or the tomato topping of the Pizza Pomodoro. Other pizza toppings vary with the seasons. You're allowed to sample each pizza before ordering one--which could be dangerous because you might end up ordering them all.

Located only a few blocks from the theater district, Sullivan Street (uptown) is a great place to grab a pre-theater light supper or snack before the show. Seating is severely restricted though. There are only two rickety chairs inside the bakery and two outside. So, if you want to sit down to enjoy your meal, take it to the theater coffee bar and devour it there. Also, if you want condiments on your pizza, you'll have to bring your own. Sullivan Street doesn't furnish any of the extra seasonings that conventional pizza parlors do.

Vegans should watch out for the Zucchini Pizza, it's topped with appetizing Zucchini morsels, but below the top layer is a subcutaneous layer of cheese. And the Tortes are all made with butter. It pays to inquire about the ingredients before biting into anything here.

See other location in Soho.

ZENITH [ve]

Full service
Asian vegetarian
$5-7.45; $12-$24 (all major cards)
No alcohol

311 West 48th Street
bet. 8th/9th Avenues
212-262-8080
daily 11:30am-11:00pm

The zenith of Chinese vegetarian cooking, this restaurant may not be--that distinction belongs to Tien Garden and The Greens--but the portions are generous, the food is tasty and any restaurant that has Zen as the first syllable of its name and serves distinguished vegetarian food is a welcome companion to Zen Palate (on which its name plays) in the theater district. Try the Grilled Marinated (mock) Vegetarian Duck as an appetizer, the Succulent Paradise (soybean Gluten marinated in a tasty barbecue sauce) as a main course and your palate will reach its zenith for the day. Dessert portions are rather small, which should suit the calorie-conscious dieter. Vegans: watch out for dairy and honey in desserts.

ZEN PALATE [ve]

Full service
Asian vegetarian
$5-7.45; $12-$24 (all major cards)
No alcohol

663 Ninth Avenue
at 46th Street
212-582-1669
daily 11:30am-10:45pm

One of our favorites, this is really two restaurants in one: upstairs, three stunning dining rooms with coppered walls, black lacquered wood trim, and tuxedoed waiters, where dinner is an elegant, expensive masterpiece in delicate, inventive cuisine; you choose between a view of Ninth Avenue, or sitting cross-legged on embroidered cushions. Downstairs, there's a simplified menu and lower prices in a café setting. Go for Dumplings, Spinach Wonton Soup, Sweet & Sour Delight with pecans and pineapple, Tofu-Chestnut Mini Loaves, Sauteed Artichoke...also vegan and dairy desserts. Besides eggs and croissants at breakfast, it's all vegan. Don't miss it. A note of caution must be sounded for vegans: some dishes contain egg products and casein.

See other location at Midtown East

The eating of animal flesh extinguishes the great seed of compassion

THE BUDDHA (SIDDHARTHA GAUTAMA OR SHAKYAMUNI) 563 BC-483 BC from *The Mahaparinirvana*

SIVANANDA YOGA VEDANTA CENTERS
EST. 1964

SIVANANDA YOGA

−FIRST CLASS FREE−

Daily Yoga Classes-all levels

- Beginners Courses
- Meditation Instruction
- Positive Thinking
- Vegetarian Meals
- Yoga Vacations
- Yoga Teachers Training

"Health is Wealth, Peace of Mind is Happiness, Yoga Shows the Way." −Swami Vishnu Devananda

Yoga Center
243 West 24th St.
New York, NY
212.255.4560
newyork@sivananda.org

Yoga Ranch
P.O. 195 Budd Rd.
Woodbourne, NY
845.436.6492
yogaranch@sivananda.org

www.sivananda.org

MIDTOWN EAST and Gramercy Park
(East 14th to East 59th Streets)

BODY AND SOUL[ve]

Food stand
International, organic
$4.00-6.00 (no cards)
No alcohol

Union Square Farmer's Market
at East 17th Street
212-982-5870
M, F 8am-6pm

One of the best ways to keep body and soul together in the city is to have a light vegan meal at the vegan food stand in the Union Square market, which is called aptly enough Body and Soul. Started by the owners of Counter restaurant back in 1994, it draws throngs of hungry folk for breakfast, lunch, early light suppers, and snacks. And it's not hard to see why. The out-size wraps and turnovers are quite toothsome. Try the Saffron Potato wrap which teases the palate with plantain chunks hidden inside. Or try the Spinach Portabello Turnover, which is filled with tofu ricotta, and tastes a bit like a Spinach Lasagna. You might want to complement this with a dairy-free Blueberry Muffin, or a Sweet Potato Muffin. Don't leave the stand without biting into a melt-in-your-mouth Chocolate Brownie, or a Wheat-Free Almond Cookie. Then repair to one of the benches in Union Square Park and have an *al fresco* meal.

See other location in Brooklyn.

BONOBOS [ve]

Self service
Organic living food, kosher
$5.95-15.95 (all cards)
No alcohol

18 East 23rd Street
bet. Park Avenue/Broadway
212-505-1200
M-Sa 11:30am-8pm

A vegetarian oasis on the E 23rd Street fast food alley, Bonobo's is a unique and delightful deli-style restaurant, serving mostly organic 100% vegan and 100% raw fruits, vegetables, nuts, and seeds. Dine on freshly made, tasty preparations under a huge skylight amid lots of plants. Or order lunch or dinner to go and take it to Madison Park across the street. In any event, the friendly staff will let you sample any prepared food to your heart's content. The prices are very reasonable and there is always a good selection of salads and fresh dressings, nut pates, soups, raw "ice- cream," puddings, and more. Everything is made on the premises with the freshest ingredients. Because Bonobo's food is not cooked it retains the maximum nutritional value and good taste.

Bonobos are awesome healthy pleasure-loving primates who are closest to humans, closer than chimpanzees. Their natural, instinctive diet is primarily fruits vegetables nuts and seeds. Who needs the diet doctors? Bonobs's is kosher and is under strict rabbinical supervision.

CHENNAI GARDEN[v]

Full service
Kosher South Indian / Punjabi
$5.95-13.95 (all cards)
No alcohol

129 East 27th Street
bet. Park/ Lexington Avenues
212-689-1999
Tu-F 11:30am-10pm
Sa, Su 12pm-10pm

Back in the late 1980s, Pradeep Shinde and Neil Constance, the two owners of this Curry Hill eatery, were among the first to open a kosher Indian vegetarian restaurant in New York. They were so successful that they retired to Orlando to take a flyer in the resort hotel business. They were successful there too, but they found that they pined for the fast tempo of New York City. So much so that they decided to collaborate on another kosher Indian vegetarian restaurant-- despite the heated competition.

Their new joint venture is called Chennai Garden. The garden is a mere figure of speech (a row of plants that borders the front window), but Chennai is the pre-colonial name of Madras, the cultural capital of South India. And the restaurant breathes the pre-colonial spirit of South India before the Raj, when flesh food was an anomaly. Our palates were tickled by the Tamarind Pullao (rice perfumed with Tamarind and peanuts), the Bhindi Masala (okra curry) and the Behl Puri (a piquant mix of puffed rice, crisped noodles, onion and cilantro). In a nod to veganism, the Gulab Jamun, a flan which is usually made with powdered milk is made here with a powdered non-dairy mock milk. This makes Chennai garden the only Kosher Indian vegetarian restaurant where one may savor a vegan version of a traditional Indian dessert. The all-you-can-eat lunch buffet for $6.95 is one of New York's best restaurant bargains.

DOSA HUT [v]

Full service
South Indian, kosher
$5.95-$6.95 (MC, V, AE)
No alcohol

102 Lexington Avenue
bet. 27th/ 28th Streets
212-725-7466
daily 12pm-10pm

The founding chef at the popular vegetarian restaurant Pongal, Virapam, has moved a few doors down the block to start his own restaurant. All the culinary artistry that he exhibited at Pongal--and which helped put it on the gastronomic map, is on display at Dosa Hut. When one of his paper thin dosas arrives in the room it creates a stir. Thin as expensive stationery and brown as a betel nut, the crisp curling disc made of rice and lentil batter is filled with a dollop of mildly spiced potatoes and onions. On the platter next to it sits a little potful of tamarind-sweet sambar (a relish) and a little pot of coconut chutney for dipping. Tear off a swatch of dosa, fill it with the spicy mashed potatoes and dip it into the sambar or the coconut chutney. To the taste it is crunchy, yielding, pungent, sweet, earthy and fiery. All for only $5.95! It is one of New York's honest bargains. An even bigger bargain is the all-you-can-eat buffet, which is served daily from 12pm to 3 pm! If the food has a homestyle flavor, it's because the chef has hired both his wife, Poonmathi, and his daughter, Jayanthi, to cook with him in the kitchen. Their dosas are so generous as to form a meal by themselves. So the judicious diner will split a dosa with his or her table mate to make room for the delicious curries such as the Bhindi Masala (Okra), Channa Masala (Chick pea), Tuver Baingen (Eggplant). The vegan might want to top off the meal with a Coconut Soup or a Mashed Potato and Broccoli soup, or even a Samosa; for the desserts, as in most Indian restaurants, are lacto-vegetarian, but not vegan.

FRANCHIA [ve]

Full Service
Korean -Western fusion
$8.95-16.95 (all cards)
Oriental & Western Wines and Beers

12 Park Avenue
bet. 34th/ 35th Streets
212-213-1001
daily 11am-10pm

William and Terri Choi, the owners of Hangawi, have opened a tea house on Park avenue and 34th street that rivals Hangawi in elegance. Its name, Franchia, means "free, lavish and generous." Decorated to look like the interior of a Korean country tea house, it provides a refuge from the turmoil and hubbub of the city, where one may sip one's tea in a Zen-like zone of tranquillity. Since we happen not to be tea drinkers, it is important to emphasize that one can dine very spaciously here and not drink a drop of tea. But, for those who love tea, Franchia is a tea shrine where one may choose from a wide selection of exotic teas, many of which are purported to have medicinal powers. Try 1st Picked Korean Wild Green Tea from the rocky slopes of Mt. Jilee, or 2nd Picked Mt. Guhwa Green Tea. There is a fixed price Royal Tea Tray, and a Zen Tea Tray. For those who prefer herbal teas, there is Mixed Herbal Tea, a Ginger Tea, a Date Paste Tea, or a Korean Plum Tea.

We chose to consume our tea as a food rather than as a beverage, so we started with Green Tea Pancakes, which were quite yummy. For a main course, we had the Sautéed Soy and Grain Meat With Asparagus and a side order of Green Tea Noodles. Also very yummy. For dessert, we had their incomparable Soy Cheese Cake with a dollop of Raspberry Sorbet.

HANGAWI [ve]

Full service
Korean
$8.95-19.95
All cards
Oriental & Western Wines and Beers

12 East 32nd Street
bet. Fifth/ Madison Avenues
212-213-0077 (reservations essential)
M-F 11am-3pm, 5pm-10:30pm
Sa 11am-10:30pm, Su 12pm to 10pm

Unless you've spent time in a Korean Buddhist monastery run by Alice Waters, you've never had food like this before. Slip off your shoes, enter a zone of absolute harmony with the sounds of rushing wind and water filling the air, and prepare to be confounded by the menu: grilled lanceolata? Ginseng in a stone bowl? Pumpkin porridge? Date paste tea? The best way to cope with this unfamiliar collection of mountain roots and greens is to order the Emperor's Meal bringing you a sample of such variety most Koreans have never tasted it. The service is impeccable and the flavors are a wonderful assortment of surprises. The owners of this superlative restaurant, William and Terri Choi, are devout Buddhists who come by their ethical vegetarian or vegan philosophy naturally. They are noted for their support of vegetarian and animal rights causes as much as for their devotion to the highest standards in food preparation and service.

MADRAS MAHAL [v]

Full service
Indian vegetarian, kosher

104 Lexington Avenue
bet. 27th/28th Streets
212-684-4010

$5.95-10.95 (major cards, $20 min)　　　　　　　Su 12pm-10pm, F 11:30am-3pm
Beer & wine　　　　　　　　　　　　　　　　M-Th 11:30am-3pm & 5:30pm-10pm

The menu asks for your patience since the food is freshly prepared. Maybe that includes scything the wheat for chapatis. At any rate, it took 45 minutes to get drinks and an hour for samosas--which were hot and flaky, with the rich taste of freshly-ground spices. After another half-hour we got Kala Chana (black chick pea curry) and Sukhi Bhaji (potato stir fried with hot pepper, dry fruit and nuts). But we were cranky after waiting so long, and the dishes didn't measure up to our expectations, especially at nine dollars apiece.

PONGAL[v]

Full service
Indian vegetarian
$6.95-9.95 (major cards)
No alcohol

110 Lexington Avenue
bet. 27th and 28th St.
212-696-9458
M-Th 11:30am-10pm
F-Su 11:30am-10:30pm

Yes, the Big Apple boasts some of the finest Indian vegetarian cuisine this side of the Indus River. Night after night, one can eat in one great Indian restaurant after another without feeling that one has dined redundantly. The dining experience at Pongal is incomparable. Start with appetizers called Kachoori, then progress to a roll-your-own-crepe called Paper Dosa. This is a large Indian crepe made of rice flour and served with spiced potato on the side. The trick to rolling your own crepe is to tear off bits of dosa; fill them with the spicy potato mixture then dip them into a fresh coconut chutney. All dishes are served on banana leaves. *Undhiya* a Gujarati dish that we sampled is highly recommended containing as it does such exotic ingredients as yam, lotus root, potatoes and eggplant. When we'd polished off this and the okra-tomato curry, the waiter brought us Kachooris (deep-fried puffs of Toor dal lentil and Bathata Dada). We finished the meal with a decaf coffee from Madras. We forbore to have any of the tempting desserts as none (alas! alack!) was vegan.

See other location at Upper East Side.

PURE FOOD AND WINE (ve)

Full service
Gourmet raw food
$17.00-23.00 (all cards)
Organic beer & wines

54 Irving Place
bet. 17th/ 18th Streets
212-477-1010
M-Su 12pm-3pm
M-Su 5:30pm-11pm

With the opening of Pure Food and Wine the preparation of rawfood has reached its apogee in New York, if not the world. The food, which is 100% vegan and raw, shows off the virtuosity of two talented New York chefs--Sarma Melngailis and Matthew Kenney (formerly of Matthews on the Upper East Side). In previous incarnations, both had won fame as *chefs de cuisine* cooking animal flesh for carnivores. But suddenly, about two years ago, over dinner at the rawfoods restaurant Quintessence, they had a simultaneous epiphany; they realized that eating vegan rawfood was better for their health, better for the health of animals, and better for the ecological health of the planet. Hence their motto, which they proudly display on the front page of their menu: "Handcrafted flavors that rejuvenate the body, mind, and planet."

A hard-bitten skeptic might scoff that chefs who excelled at making dead animal parts taste yummy should have no trouble infusing raw vegetable and fruit concoctions with flavor. Just so. This is why the food at Pure Food and Wine surpasses that of any other rawfood restaurant that we have visited. These two chefs have applied the *hautest* techniques of *nouvelle cuisine* to the preparation of rawfoods, and the results are truly sensational.

We can unreservedly recommend all the dishes that we tasted. Start with the Thai Lettuce Wraps that come with a spicy tamarind dipping sauce. Another appetizer to try is the Tomato Tartare with Kaffir Lime. For a main course, try the Beet Ravioli--[Rectangles of thinly sliced beets sandwiched together with a cashew nut filling]. Or the Golden Squash Pasta with Summer Black Truffles [Spiralized Yellow Squash slathered with a hearty truffle sauce with sweet peas and chervil]. For dessert, we commend to your tastebuds Chewy Dark Chocolate Cookie with Chocolate and Pistachio Ice Creams [This is a soft cookie, served with candied pistachios, strawberry sauce, and dollops of vegan ice-cream made from nut cream.]

The restaurant's interior is plush, and the walls are decorated with pictures of happy animals (pleased, no doubt, because they're not being eaten). The spacious patio is the perfect setting for the eating of things raw. Here one may dine *al fresco,* and in the event of a sudden downpour waiters are adept at setting up huge parasols that protect the diners from precipitation. The atmosphere is so convivial that strangers talk to each other across tables. Sitting next to us were two non-vegetarian women who were prolonging their meal by ordering endless glasses of coconut water and organic wine--because they couldn't tear themselves away from the place. It's that magnetic!

Not content to rest on their laurels, Kenney and Melngailis have collaborated on an uncook book, *Raw Food/ Real World: 100 Recipes to Get the Glow,* which tells one how to reconstruct the dishes that are on offer in the restaurant. Published by Regan Books, it promises well to be a bestseller. Early in 2006, Sharma and Matthew parted ways. Sharma continues to run Pure Food with her customary élan and Matthew has gone on to start a chain of rawfood cafes called Blue Green. He has also founded a rawfood preparation center--the Plant in Dumbo--where he gives personal instruction in the making of rawfood dishes.

PURE JUICE AND TAKE AWAY (ve)

Full Service
Gourmet raw food
$4.00-12.00 (all cards)
No alcohol

125 1/2 East 17th Street
bet. 3rd Avenue/ Irving Place
212-477-7151
daily 11am-11pm

This is the vest-picket version of Pure Food and Wine with many of the menu items at PFW available for take-out. Here, you can get one of Pure Food's tastiest dishes, the Heirloom Tomato Lasagna with Basil Pesto and Pignoli Ricotta. Their Flatbread Pizza with Hummus, Avocado and Mint Pesto makes a delectable take away lunch, as does our favorite Tortilla Wrap with Chili Spiced 'Beans' The juice bar offers some exotic juice combinations such as Hot Pink (Beet Pineapple, Watermelon and Ginger) and smoothies. Try the Mango Shake (Mango, Fresh Coconut Water and a dash of Vanilla). Many of the desserts served at Pure Food are also offered here. We were glad to see the Toco Coco Brownies. And we also liked the Fruit, Granola and Vanilla Cream Parfait. The desserts, as at Pure Food, are made without honey. Making a commendable effort to be consistently vegan, they use Agave Nectar and Maple Syrup instead of honey.

SARAVANA BHAVANA (v)

Full service
Chennai homestyle
$6.25-13.95 (major cards)
Wine & beer

81 Lexington Avenue
at 26th Streets
212-679-0204
Lunch Tu-Su 12m-4pm
Dinner 5:30pm-10pm

Saravana Bhavan--Englished means "house of Saravana". Brother of Ganesh, the elephant god of prosperity, Sarvana seems to be shedding a benign protection on this house. And according to the manager, Ms. Ramaya, they will need every ounce of Saravanaas' help. There is fierce competition with other Indian restaurants on Curry Hill, and there appears to be a jinx on the street corner where Saravanaas is located.. So far, every restaurant that has occupied this corner has failed.

But if the quality of the food and the service are anything to go by, Saravanaas will beat the odds. Already, the place is packed with frugal diners, both Indian and Western, who obviously recognize a bargain when they eat one. Modestly priced, and highly flavorsome, the cuisine-- Chennai homestyle--is the type of food that one might encounter at a home in Chennai (formerly Madras). The menu abounds in delicious dosas, uthapams, vadas, and thalis redolent of India's deep south. Nearly all the dishes are cooked in oil, not ghee (clarified butter). But vegans must beware of the Iddly (Steamed Rice and Lentil Patty), which is topped off with a ladleful of ghee. Also, the Sambars in the Thalis are sometimes flavored with ghee.

For an appetizer, we had the Sambar Vada (Crispy Lentil Doughnuts in a Mild, Spicy South Indian Soup, Garnished with Onion and Cilantro). For the main course, we had the Dried Fruit Rava Dosa (a mildly spiced Crepe made of Wheat and Rice Flour, blended with Whole Raisins, Pistachios, and Cashews). This we dipped into three different coconut-based chutneys and a sambar. Verboten to vegans are the desserts. As in most Indian restaurants, they are highly caseous, containing ghee, milk, yogurt, and cheese.

Unlike other restaurants on Curry Hill, Saravanaas refuses to use frozen vegetables and will not serve leftovers. Ms. Ramaya told us that all the vegetables are purchased from local Indian suppliers. This accounts for the high quality and astonishing freshness of each dish. Saravan Bhavan is actually the New York branch franchise of a chain of successful Indian vegetarian restaurants that originate in Chennai. So all the dishes are made to standards set by the home office in Chennai. This can have its drawbacks. When we asked for soy milk to be used in a Lassi, or in an Indian coffee, which is pre-mixed with cow's milk, the manager told us that the home office does not permit its franchises to substitute soy milk for cow's milk. This strikes us as a silly practice-- especially as the home office has allowed the New York franchise to serve wine and beer, which no other restaurant in the chain is allowed to do. So, it is incumbent that vegans politely demand soy milk for their lassis and coffees.[If the Starbucks chain,--which is non-veg.-- can offer soymilk, then why not Saravana Bhavana, which is veg.?] Apart from this notable lapse, the service is faultless, and the food is very good value for the money.

VATAN [v]

Full service
Indian
$24.95 prix fixe (V, MC)
Full bar

409 Third Avenue
at 29th Street
212-689-5666 (reservations essential)
Tu-Su 5:30pm-11pm
Closed Mondays

At first glance, $22.95 prix fixe may seem like a lot of rupees, but think of a visit to Vatan as a cut-price ticket to India. The decor instantly transports you to a village in Gujarat, where costumed waiters and waitresses look as if they've just popped out of Aladdin's lamp to do your bidding. At the snap of your fingers, they will bring you all the appetizers you can eat; and the appetizers are so indescribably scrumptious, you'll eat yourself into a stupor. We stuffed ourselves unashamedly with delicate miniature samosas filled with peas and potatoes, the Chana Masala (chick peas with onions and coriander) and an array of Indian breads such as papadams and puris, but still found room for a rich dessert of Mango Rus (mango pulp). The music, authentic Indian ragas, is soft and unobtrusive. The food is prepared with canola oil, not ghee. The service is faultless.

ZEN PALATE [v]

Full service
Asian vegetarian
$5-7.45; $12-$24 (all major cards)
No alcohol

34 East Union Square
at 16th Street
212-614-9345
Upstairs: daily 11:30a-3& 5:30p-11p
Downstairs: M-Sa 7a-11p, Su 12p-11p

One of our favorites, this is really two restaurants in one: upstairs, three stunning dining rooms with coppered walls, black lacquered wood trim, and tuxedoed waiters, where dinner is an elegant, expensive masterpiece in delicate, inventive cuisine; you choose between a view over Union Square or sitting cross-legged on embroidered cushions. Downstairs, there's a simplified menu and lower prices in a café setting. Go for Dumplings, Spinach Wonton Soup, Sweet & Sour Delight with pecans and pineapple, Tofu-Chestnut Mini Loaves, Sauteed Artichoke...also vegan and dairy desserts. Besides eggs and croissants at breakfast, it's all vegan. Don't miss it. A note of caution must be sounded for vegans: some dishes contain egg products and casein.

See other locations at Midtown West and Upper West Side.

Great Tasting Vegan Dairy-Free Gourmet

Chocolate Decadence

Log on to our website at
www.chocolatedecadence.com
or Call us for a free brochure
Toll-free at
1-800-324-5018

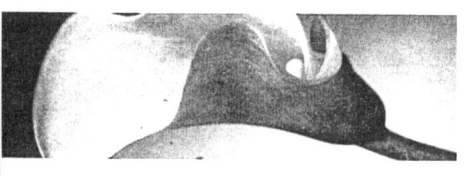

BLOSSOM
organic vegan cuisine
187 Ninth Avenue
New York City
(212) 627-1144
www.blossomnyc.com

> I have from an early age abjured the use of meat, and the time will come when men such as I will look upon the murder of animals as they now look upon the murder of men.

LEONARDO DA VINCI, 1452-1519
Artist. scientist. inventor, engineer, architect, "Renaissance Man"

GREENWICH VILLAGE
(Houston Street to West 14th Street, Hudson River to Fifth Avenue)

APPLE RESTAURANT [v]

Full service
Vegetarian and mixed Vietnamese
$5.95-8.95 (AE,MC,V)
Full bar

17 Waverly Place
at Greene Street
212-473-8888
M-Th 11am-11pm
F-Sa 11am-12am Su 11am-10pm

A vast dining room with a cathedral ceiling, horseshoe bar and white tablecloths, large enough to encompass several different styles: one menu is mixed Vietnamese cuisine and the other is mostly vegan natural fare, from the Middle East to Mexico by way of Japan. Consistent high quality and a classy setting despite the karaoke (sing-a-long) room hidden in the back. Jazz singers croon sweetly on weekend nights. Mouthwatering desserts free of honey and dairy are worth the trip alone.

EAST-WEST CAFE [v]

Self service
Organic Asian-Western cuisine
$8.00-15.00 (all cards)
Organic beer & wine
www.eastwestnyc.com

78 Fifthavenue
bet. 13th/ 14thStreets
212--243-3667
dairly 10am-9pm

By the time it closed its doors for good in November 2005, the old East West bookstore--an endearingly shabby esoteric book shop--must have laid up masses of good karma in its checkered life. For now, under the new ownership of Jan Matthews, it has attained a much higher incarnation as an elegantly designed metaphysical book shop with a spiffy new cafe upstairs--the East West Cafe.

Chad Currier, the manager of the East West Cafe, said that he tried to make the cafe "a culinary manifestation of the spirit of the bookstore." In this he has succeeded admirably. The space fairly exhales spirituality.

Poised above the bookstore, on the cloud-like mezzanine floor, we ate our meal while we gazed down on the patrons below--as if we were lesser Hindu deities. Speaking of deities--gorgeous pen and ink drawings illustrating mythological scenes from the Mahabharata, the Ramayana, and other Indian epics, grace the cafe's walls. [Copies of these drawings are for sale.]

Suitably enough, many of the main dishes have Sanskrit names as if the very act of consuming them were an act of devotion. We had a delicious Capanata Salad (triple-washed spinach, alfalfa sprouts, vine-ripe tomatoes, grilled eggplant, garbanzos, roasted garlic, oil-cured olives) followed by a Tuscan Roasted Vegetable Sandwich that featured roasted eggplant sun-dried tomato, triple-washed spinach, organic apple, and basil on seven-grain bread. To accompany it, we sipped the most delicious
Soy Chai (black tea, soymilk with agave nectar, and Indian masala).

After eating to repletion, we pursued one of our favorite postprandial pastimes--browsing in a bookstore. Only now we had but to descend the staircase to have a browse in New York's best metaphysical bookstore. Although the cafe upstairs is meant to be subservient to the bookstore--its food is so appealing, and its space so seductively designed, that eventually it may upstage the bookstore to become a destination for vegan gourmets.

GOBO [ve]

Full service
Organic, Asian-Western fusion cuisine
$8.00-15.00 (all cards)
Organic beer & wine
www.goborestaurant.com

402 Sixth Avenue
at 8th Street
212-255-3242
Su-We 11:30am-11:30pm
Th-Sa 11:30am-12am

The atmosphere of Gobo-- the Japanese word for the root vegetable, burdock--is reminiscent of the tastefully decorated Zen Palate restaurants. The comparison is entirely appropriate because the owners of Gobo, Darryn and David Wu are the sons of the owners of Zen Palate, Mr. and Mrs. Tiehjyh Wu. Just as Zen Palate invokes the influence of Buddhism as their *raison d' etre*, so there is a statue of the Buddha prominently displayed at Gobo; he is smiling his blessing upon Gobo food, which is faithful to the Buddha's first precept of *ahimsa* (non-violence to all living creatures).

Gobo is proof of the fact that one can be a principled vegetarian yet enjoy the most exquisite food. For the food at Gobo's outstrips the cuisine of its parent restaurant Zen Palate. (This is ironic because most of the dishes were created by Mrs. Wu, the co-owner of Zen Palate). We started our dinner with a smoothie called The Awakening (mango, cherry and wolfberry), which was truly ambrosial. With our taste buds duly awakened, we were in a fit condition to enjoy the entrees, which were also very much to our taste--Sizzling Soy Cutlet Platter with Black Pepper Sauce, and the Soy Filet with Coconut Curry Rice. The desserts, all of which are vegan, were also extraordinary. We relished the Multi-layered Chocolate Cake and the Coconut-Chocolate Pudding with Mango Puree.

There are two non-vegan dishes--Avocado Tartare, which contains honey; and Crispy Spinach and Soy Cheese Wontons, which contains casein, a cows' milk extract, and egg, an ingredient in the won ton wrappers. Cow's milk, alas, is also available to tea and coffee drinkers who prefer it to the soy milk that is on offer.

The talk is that, if it is successful, Gobo plans to franchise the restaurant. Judging from the impeccable service, the attractive decor and the exquisite food, the burdock will soon be taking root in other American cities.

See other location in Upper East Side.

HUMMUS PLACE [v]

Full Service
Israeli vegetarian, kosher
$4.50-5.95 (all cards)
Wine & Beer

99 Macdougal Street
bet. W. 3rd/ Bleecker Streets
212-533-3089
Su-Th 11am-12am
Fr-Sa 11am-2am

New York already has single-food-item restaurants dedicated to the French Fry, the Falafel, the

Baked Potato, the Crepe, the Dosa, the Pancake, the Doughnut, Popcorn, Soup, and the Noodle; there is even a Candy bar (Dylan's)--so why not a restaurant devoted soley to Hummus? At Hummus Place, a tidy little beanery with walls the color of tahini, you can order two different styles of hummus--one made from fava beans and chickpeas, Hummus Foul (pronounced fool), and the other made from whole chickpeas, Hummus Masabacha. The fava beans and the chickpeas are imported from Israel to insure quality and freshness. The beans are then set to soak overnight and are chopped up in a huge Robotcoupe; then cooked for a full five hours. The hummus is served with a snow white tahini which is also imported from Israel.Two of the dishes are made with eggs; so vegans must tell the chef to hold the eggs!

Fittingly enough, the man who founded Hummus Place is an Israeli named Ori Apple, formerly of Kibbutz Maoz Haim. After his army service in Israel, Apple alighted in the Big Apple to study cooking at the French Culinary Institute in Soho. Having worked for a number of restaurants and a catering service in the city, Apple decided to strike out on his own. With the help and advice of his best friend--(now co-owner and chef of Hummus Place)--Nitzan Raz, Apple started Hummus Place. Apple's hummus is considered to be so authentic that Israelis joke that they no longer have any reason to visit Tel Aviv.

Because they've been cooked to a fare-thee-well-well, the flavor of the hummuses are a bit bland. Luckily, they come with a hot sauce on the side with a secret recipe whose base is cilantro. We found that the judicious seasoning of hummus with hot sauce enlivens the flavor and makes it go down much better. The hummus also comes with an Israeli Salad (whose ingredients are not imported from Israel). To give it an added fillip, we tried mixing the Israeli Salad in with the hummus and the hot sauce Then we used; the resultant mixture to fill a whole wheat pita pocket, which came with our order. This worked splendidly. We washed it all down with a cool glass of refreshing lemonade (also made with a secret recipe) that contains a sprig of fresh Israeli Mint. At the end of our meal, we left feeling satisfied and full of beans.

See other location under East Village.

INTEGRAL YOGA NATURAL FOODS [ve]

Take-out counter
International
$4.00-7.00 (all cards)
No alcohol
www. iynaturalfoods.com

229 West 13th Street
bet. 7th/ 8th Avenues
212-243-2642
M-F 9am-9:30pm
Sa-Su 9-8:30pm

Integral Yoga was started by Swami Satchidananda back in the seventies. The Swami taught that it was bad karma to consume or purvey animal flesh. Consequently, Integral Yoga is one of the few health food stores in the city that doesn't peddle flesh. Now you can tap into their good karma by having a meal there. Nestled into the North West corner of the store is one of the city's best vegan buffets. You may choose from such selections as Curried Black-Eyed Peas, Hot and Spicy Tofu and Bokchoy with Almonds. There is also a juice bar where you may purchase soups and veggie burgers If you're a rawfoodist, take heart! There a capacious salad bar, and in a refrigerated display case next to the buffet, there is an appetizing selection of raw vegetable pies, fruit pies, cakes, and cookies.

NEW YORK DOSAS[ve]

Food cart
South Indian
$5.00-7.00 (no cards)
No alcohol

Washington Square Park
West 4th/ Sullivan Streets
917-710-2092
M-Sa 11am-5pm

We had to stand in line behind ten people to give our order to Thiru Kumar , the chef who works his magic at this outdoor food cart. Our order was for a Masala Dosa (a rolled rice-flour crepe stuffed with spicy potato mixture), Jafna Dosa (a rolled rice-flour crepe stuffed with Sambahl); Ponidicherry Utapam (a flat bread topped with fresh, chopped vegetables); and Iddly with Sambar (an Indian biscuit made from lentil flour and dipped in a spicy Sambar or soup).

Thiru, a native of Sri Lanka, works fast; he pours a batter made from crushed fermented rice and lentils on the griddle and within a few seconds, Utapam and Dosas appear, as if by magic. He fills them with spicy mashed potatoes and chopped fresh vegetables--and the result dosas and utapams worthy of the finest Indian restaurants.

Thiru packed our order into boxes; then we sat on a bench in Washington Square park and savored every morsel.

It's hard to believe that so much food can pour forth from one little food cart! In addition to the Dosas, one may order Samosas with vegetable fillings; Medhu Vada (lentil donuts), and the aforementioned Iddly with Sambar. Thiru also offers up a unique array of tinned fruit juices imported from Thailand--such as Rambutan juice, Longan juice, and, our favorite, Lychee juice-- that are available nowhere else in the city. Unusual for an Indian food establishment, vegans may dine here without having to ask about objectionable ingredients--as all the food is 100 per cent vegan. [Thiru bowed to pressure from vegan students at the NYU Vegan Society to make his food cart exclusively vegan. Now he himself has turned vegan.]

RED BAMBOO [ve]

Full service
Asian soul food fusion
$9.95-12.95 (all cards)
No alcohol
www.redbamboo-nyc.com

140 West 4th Street
bet. 6th/MacDougal
212-260-1212
M-F 4pm-12am
Sa-Su 12pm-12am

"Soul Food with Asian overtones" is how the proprietor, Jason Wong, the son, of the owners of VP2, describes the cuisine At play here are multi-ethnic flavors such as Chinese, Korean, Thai, Indian. Creole and Soul Food. In most instances, the fusion of flavors works.

For appetizers, we had the Jerk Spiced Seitan, which was tangy and tasty, as were the Deep-Fried Butterfly Shrimp, and the gluten "pork" in the Tonkatsu Chops. We also sampled the Tandoori Chicken Supreme. and Buffalo Wings, which were finger lickin' good. However, on the debit side, the Seoul Pancake was too mushy and the sweet corn mashed potatoes were way too bland. We capped it all off with a scrumptious Chocolate Peanut Butter Cake served with a dollop of vegan Mint Chocolate Chip ice-cream. The waiters were attentive and hovering.

The only difficulty that vegans might have with eating at Red Bamboo is that the menu is so unrelievedly mock-carnivorous that the mere sight of dishes with names like Tandoori Chicken,

Shrimp, and Salmon, no matter how mock, might conjure unpleasant associations with the real thing. Nonethless, Red Bamboo is a great place to take your meat-eating friends to show them how animal flesh may be mocked to perfection. Two dishes contain dairy and these are noted on the menu.

See other location in Brooklyn

SACRED CHOW [v]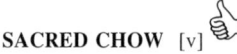

Full service
International & bakery
$4-8 (V, AE, MC)
Organic beer & wine
www.sacredchow.com

227 Sullivan Street
bet. West 3rd & Bleecker Streets
212-337-0863
M-F 9 am--11pm
Sa-Su 11:30am-11pm

Cliff Preefer, the owner of Sacred Chow used to be the head chef as well as the pastry chef, at Candle Cafe back in the mid-90's. Then he decided to strike out on his own and start a veg. delicatessen, which eventually gave place to this new restaurant of the same name. Casting about for a name for his eatery, he hit upon the inspired pun--"sacred chow." With its logo of the meditating cow, and its pun on sacred cow, could Cliff's restaurant have been anything but vegan? Unfortunately, yes. Cliff does serve dairy products in the shape of ice-cream and creamers for coffee. This is rather a desecration of that poor sacred cow, who is exploited for its exudate, is it not?
    Apart from this notable lapse, there is an admirable respect for the cow that pervades the restaurant and its menu. There are usually about thirty vegan tapas on offer. The ones we sampled were extraordinary--Korean Tofu Cutlets, the Shredded Tofu Spa Salad, and Curried Steamed Broccoli. The Hero Sandwich that we had as a main course --Roasted Black Olive Seitan, with molten vegan Mozzarella --was so good that we had to stifle a shout of jubilation. [Fact is: Cliff's Hero sandwiches and pastries are so sought-after that he retails them to other snackeries around the city--like the one in the cafe at the Angelika Cinema.]
    While we munched our Heroes, amid the warm, rouge tints of the interior decor, we sipped one of Cliff's frozen smoothies, which he calls Gym Body (bananas, toasted almonds, cinnamon, flax oil and apple juice). This was so satisfyig that we could easily have made a meal of it.
    For dessert we inhaled Cliff's famous Velvet Triple Chocolate Brownie with a side scoop of organic vegan Raspberry Ice-Cream. Cliff, [excuse the bad pun], we will be dropping over quite often, (especially if S. C. becomes 100% vegan)!

Indicates we especially recommend this restaurant for the quality of the food.

'sNICE [v]

Self service
Sandwiches, salads, baked goods
$4.00-7.00 (all cards)
Beer & wine

45 8th Avenue
at 4th Street
212-645-0310
daily 7:30am-10pm

'sWonderful, 'sMarvelous, 'sNice? You'll surely agree that this coffee shop-cum-bistro deserves a loftier superlative than merely nice. Really, the food is nothing short of S'Marvelous! Their funky-tasting sandwiches--the Vegetable Pot Pie Wrap, the Vegan Panini with Smoked Tofu Pesto Sun-Dried Tomatoes, and the Curried Cauliflower with Chickpea Wrap [There is even a chocolate vegan ice-cream sandwich pressed between two of Deb's home-baked chocolate chip cookies]--so bewitch the palate as to smack of sandwitchcraft. If the baked goods taste home-baked, it's because they're baked on the premises by Deborah, the wife of Michael, the founder. A decade-and-a-half as the owner of a string of Greenwich Village cabarets have stood Michael in good stead. He's acquired the street smarts to know where to find the best strawberry lemonade, the best fizzy waters(Izzi grapefruit and pear); the best soft drinks (Cane Colas that taste as soft drinks from the fifties used to taste when they were made with cane sugar instead of high fructose corn syrup.).

Michael's sunny demeanor belies his years in the benighted nightclub business. His friendly, easy-going manner allows customers to linger at their tables and peruse the free newspapers or paperback books with which the restaurant is liberally supplied. Bored to extinction? If so, Michael and Deb have thoughtfully provided a shelf full of board games like checkers, scrabble and Parcheesi to beguile away the leaden hours. [We downed our wraps while walloping each other at checkers.] For chocaholics [which includes us], there is a bowl-sized mug of vegan hot chocolate that comes with vegan marshmallows floating on top. In our culinary lexicon, 'sWonderful is a synonym for 'sNice !

VP2

Full service
Chinese
$4.95-12.95 (AE,MC,V)
No alcohol

140 / 144 West 4th Street
bet. Sixth Ave/ MacDougal Street
212-260-7130/7141
M-Th 12pm-11pm, F-Sa 12pm-12am

We know, you've long since given up ordering Peking Spare Ribs, Sweet and Pungent Pork and Squid in Black Bean Sauce. Do it anyway. The meaty names just help identify traditional Chinese dishes that VP's Buddhist chefs prepare exclusively without animal products (using soy, wheat, and arrowroot substitutes). The food is authentic and reasonably priced, served in a modern, sleek restaurant . One of the best of this type of place.

EAST VILLAGE
(Houston to East 14th Street, Fifth Avenue to the East River)

ANGELICA KITCHEN [ve]

Full service
Natural
$9.95-14.95 (no cards)
No alcohol

300 E 12th Street
at Second Avenue
212-228-2909
daily 11:30am-10:30pm

Hands down one of the best vegan restaurants anywhere. For 25 years Angelica Kitchen has set the standard for fresh organic fare with a conscience.
   Each day there are two very special, always new, special entrees such as "Here Today-- Gone Tamale'" (Festive tamales made with Iroquois white corn masa and roasted home-made seitan, chipotle and ancho chili peppers, all wrapped in a corn husk served with tomato-cilantro salsa, over a baby lima bean sauce, with baby lettuces and steamed local asparagus). Or try the norimake rolls with grilled tempeh, home-made pickled carrots and brown rice; like sushi, they're rolled in nori seaweed .
   For those who wish to try Angelica Kitchen's tasty dishes at home, the *Angelica Home Kitchen Cookbook* by Leslie McEachern (the owner) is for sale in the restaurant. It includes over 100 recipes from the menu archives that have been specially formulated for the home cook. The book also sets forth Leslie's philosophy and principles for running a socially conscious business, and it features profiles of the farmers and artisans who provide the restaurant with the ingredients for their delicious fare.
   Angelica's is a dessertatarian's delight. We swooned over the rhubarb layer cake with strawberry frosting and the coconut flan with pineapple salsa was unforgettable. Consistently fresh, flavorful and satisfying, the whole vital menu proves why the outstanding reputation of Angelica Kitchen is so richly deserved Take-out next door.

CAFE VIVA [A.K.A. **VIVA HERBAL PIZZERIA**]

Counter service
Italian, organic, kosher
$1.52-7.95 (all cards)
No alcohol

179 Second Avenue
bet. 11th / 12th Streets
212-420-8801
daily 11am-11pm
Sa-Su 11am-12am

See description under Upper West Side

CARAVAN OF DREAMS [ve]

Full service
International organic, kosher
$10.00-15.00 (V,MC)
Full bar, organic beer & wine

405 East 6th Street
bet. First Ave/Avenue A
212-254-1613
M-Su 11am-11pm, Sa 11am-12am
Sa,Su brunch 11am-5pm

Organic vegetarian food in a hippy atmosphere of long hair, mix-and-match furniture and live music almost every night. Quite relaxing during non-peak hours. No dairy is used; a few years ago, Caravan went completely vegan. Black bean chili, grilled polenta, African spinach stew over rice, pasta, burritos, quesadilla, ginger-curried stir-fry, tempeh, large salads, sandwiches, "greens of the day." A pleasure. Recently Caravan has begun serving raw-food entrees every day. It also serves a range of raw soups and desserts. Their raw broccoli soup is simply delicious, and their raw raspberry cake bears comparison with any baked cake in town. Every night, their new raw chef creates live food specials that rotate every week. We enjoyed the Taco Salad, the Live Mock Meat Balls, the Live Nachos, and the Live Sandwich. Obviously Caravan's Dreams have come to life.

COUNTER [ve]

Full Service
International, organic
$8.95-15.25
All cards
Organic wines

105 First Avenue
bet. 6th Avenue/7th Street
212-982-5870
M-F 5pm-11:30pm
Sa 11am-12am, Su 11am-11pm

Counter is a felicitous name for a vegetarian restaurant because it runs counter to the majority of restaurants in New York where dead animals are the focus of dining rituals.

Counter doesn't look counter-cultural though. The handsome interior design with its art deco accents, make it one of New York's most elegant eateries. And the food is sublime. We started with a Porccini Pizza, topped with a nut cheese which was robust and flavorful. We followed this with a Cauliflower Risotto, which were also very tasty. Then we split a Cosmo Burger, a walnut-tempeh patty that was more mundane than cosmic. The garlic-herb aioli that accompanied it was good, but the French-Fries were limp and soggy. For the main course, we recommend the Pasta with Pine Nuts, seasoned with Micro Pepper Cress, picked from Deborah, the owner's roof garden. We were lucky to have dined there on Tuesday, which was raw food night. The raw food chef, Michelle Thorne, prepared a Marinated Peach Salad that was tasty, tart, and sweet. It too was seasoned with herbs from Deborah's roof garden. The raw entree was Stuffed Zucchini Blossoms, which was as flavorful as it was inventive.. The desserts were just as successful. The Verona Chocolate Pie with Vanilla Soy Ice-Cream was eminently satisfying . and we adored their Three Berry Cake,which is topped with a rich vanilla nut cream to compound the decadence. Sad to report, when we quizzed the owners as to whether Counter was totally vegan, they said that it was. Evidently they had forgotten about the milk that they use in the cappuccino, coffees, teas, and other beverages. Deborah assured us that this was an oversight, but that they never used dairy products in any of their food preparations Nonetheless, when it comes to ordering coffee, or Tecchino, a vegan cappuccino, vegans should request soy milk substitutions.

Recently, (as of this writing), Counter has hired noted rawfoods chef, Chad Sarno, to revamp their menu. By mid-2006, Donna, the co-owner reckons that Counter's menu will be fifty-percent raw!

CURLY'S VEGETARIAN LUNCH [v]

Full Service
American fast food
$5.95-10.95 (all cards)
Beer & Sangria

328 East 14th Street
bet. 1st & 2nd Avenues
212-598-9998
Daily 11am-11pm

Rectangular in shape, with cream colored walls, decorated with two parallel mango stripes, and a lozenge-shaped mirror, there is nothing kinky about Curly's Vegetarian Lunch--except the curly French fries-and the Cubano Sandwich. They have a kinky flavor that wraps itself around your tongue and won't let go. As a rule, we don't care much for mock meat--it's too rereminiscent of the real thing--but we're making an exception for Curly's Cubano. Heaven help the folks who eat the real (carnivorous) Cubano: it has enough cholesterol to thrombose a regiment of Visigoths. But Curly's vegan Cubano with its mock ham, mock dark meat, mock cheese, sans casein, and pickle has a raffish appeal to the taste buds that is not to be denied. Ditto for the mock Buffalo wings. Both by the way are "two-hanky" specials that require two or more napkins to eat without spotting one's blouse. We also savored the Cashew Sofrito (Unsalted cashew nuts in a sofrito of tomato, peppers, olives and achiote. served over fried plantain with back beans and grain). And you don't have to go anywhere else for dessert. Curly's serves a full complement of Vegan Treats' pies and cakes that Veg-City Diner was famous for.

Curly's Vegetarian Lunch seems a quirky name for a restaurant. But a glance at the back page of the menu explains everything. There, the founders and owners of Curly's--David and Jean--have thoughtfully provided the story of how the restaurant got its name. Curly, the grandfather of David, owned a diner in New Hampshire. After a catastrophic flood washed away most of the town, Curly provided free food for the townspeople, and became a local hero. David, wanted to pay tribute to his grandfather's food as well as his unsung heroism.

We almost forgot to mention that Curly's is the brain child of David and his wife Jean, the former owners of the late-lamented Veg-City Diner, which was forced to close because of a freak kitchen fire. Neither David nor his wife is a vegetarian, but they love to prepare vegetarian food, and delight in inventing new ways to use mock meats. David is also the former owner of Burritoville, the only Mexican restaurant in New York City that has vegan sour cream; he has an abiding love affair with Mexican cuisine. His contract with the buyers of Buttitoville won't let him make Mexican food at Curly's. His vegan Cubano is an homage to the Vegan Mexican cuisine of his heart's desire. Someday, he promises to open a 100 per cent vegan Mexican restaurant. On that day, we'll be the first in line.

HUMMUS PLACE [v]

Full Service
Israeli vegetarian, kosher
$4.50-5.95 (all cards)
Wine & Beer

109 St. Marks Place
bet. 1st & A Avenues
212-529-9198
Su-Th 11am-12am
Fr-Sa 11am-2am

See description under Greenwich Village.

JIVAMUKTEA[ve] 👍

Counter service
Cosmic vegan organic,
$8.00 -12.00 (all cards)
No alcohol
www.JivamukTea.com

841 Broadway
bet. 13th/ 14th Streets
212-353-0214
daily 10am -9pm

The founders of Jivamukti Yoga, David Life and Sharon Gannon, are to be highly commended. Their spanking new Jivamukti yoga center, which opened in June 2006, is furnished with eco-friendly objects trouves, recycled tables, chairs, and flooring made from recycled car tires They've also incorporated a cafe, JivamukTea , that features exclusively vegan food. Overlooking the hubbub of Broadway, in a spacious, airy setting, with an azure ceiling, antique chandeliers, and soaring stained glass windows--JivamukTea Cafe is replete with fit-looking yogis fresh from their round of *asanas*.

Unlike most yoga ashrams, that give short shrift to the first precept of the classical systems of yoga, it is clear that Gannon and Life uphold the view of Patanjali that if one is to advance spiritually in the practice of yoga, one must eat non-violent food. In fact, in a recent interview, Sharon Gannon said, "Veganism is essential to the practice of yoga, where you do not exploit animals for any purpose. Patanjali, in the Yoga Sutra, gives *Ahimsa* (non harming of others) as the primary means to enlightenment." To that end, Life and Gannon have joined forces with veg. chef Matthew Kenney to create a menu that is conducive to attaining the higher states of yogic consciousness--and to having a darned tasty meal!

Totally vegan, the menu boasts many dishes that are often unheated or raw. Matthew Kenney's unmistakable signature is on many of the tastiest dishes such as the Opera Zone: Raw Lasagna (sun dried tomato puree, mint-basil pesto, and macadamia ricotta). Or, Soul Source (portobello tacos with mango guacamole and citrus sour cream). Or the scintillating sandwich The Creator BLT (Seitan Bacon, Baby Bibb Lettuce, Heirloom Tomato, and Chipotle Mayo on Wheat).

On a sideboard, Gannon and Life have thoughtfully provided "Finishes": containers of agave nectar, soy milk non-dairy creamer, almond milk, stevia, succanat and other vegan substitutes for condiments usually made with animal products.

Juices and smoothies bearing names of the Chakras are made in a sound-proof glass booth. Our favorite was the Root Chakra (Amazon cherry, blueberry, acai, cacao, and Brazil-nut milk).

We concluded our meal with a heavenly Raw Strawberry Cheesecake and a cup of After Yoga Tea.

When the time comes that you must depart from JivamukTea, you may be contentedly purring OM-M-m--m as well as M-M-M-m-m-m!

👍 Indicates we especially recommend this restaurant for the quality of the food.

JUBB'S LONGEVITY [ve]

Counter service
Organic Lifefood
$3.95-12.95 (V, MC)
No alcohol

508 East 12th Street
bet. Avenues A/B
212-353-5000
daily 10am -9pm

Although Jubb's Longevity is technically a deli, so many people crowd into it for lunch, brunch and dinner that we're treating it as a restaurant. The proprietor, Dr. David Jubb, is probably the only chef in New York with a Ph.D in bionutrition. But when it comes to preparing raw food, or "Lifefood," as he calls it, David is an alchemist.

By Lifefood he means food that is organic, unhybridized and uncooked. It's prepared in a way that the "life-force" remains intact, making it easily digestible. Lifefooders eat mainly fruits, nuts and seeds produced by shade-bearing plants that promote the growth of topsoil, thereby enhancing vitality of earth and self. On our last visit to Jubb's, we had the raw pizza, which consists of a sour dough pizza crust made from sprouted buckwheat (actually a seed), flaxseed and low-temperature-dried-sea vegetables, topped with Italian-flavored tomato and pesto sauce with a pine nut and pumpkin seed cheese. We chased this with a glass of cold pressed nut milk and followed that with a vegan live yogurt made from sweetsop and passion fruit for dessert. On our previous visit, we had polished off the Live Burger Deluxe, which is composed of zucchini, celery pine nuts, sprouted pumpkin seeds, sea vegetables, and dehydrated wild fruits and greens. It's served on unleavened sour dough bread on a bed of chopped greens. It comes with a raspberry mayonnaise, a pine nut seed cheese and a spicy sauce. All the ingredients of his dishes, it bears repeating, are organic and raw. For dessert, we downed an antioxidant energy bar made from rose hips, hibiscus, elderberry, papaya and lemon et al. We then chugged down an E-Z Tea whose ingredients are wolf berry, ginger, prickly ash, buck thorn bark, blessed thistle, carob and mint.

If you're a vegan ice-cream lover, and who isn't, you must taste David's Butterscotch ice-cream, which is made from raw apricots. It's an elixir, and a delight. Yes David is an alchemist of food. It's easy to see why he's the diet guru of Donna Karen and other celebrities who have gone raw. David's food is not only energizing, it's life-giving and soul-satisfying.

KATE'S JOINT [ve]

Full Service
American, organic
$5.95-7.95 (AE, MC,V)
Beer & wine

58 Avenue B
bet. 4th / 5th Streets
212-777-7059
Su-W 8:30 am-11pm
Th-Sa 8am-12pm

Eating at Kate's Joint is like stepping into a Norman Rockwell painting from the fifties. The food as well as the atmosphere are faux fifties--a time when restaurants were called "joints", coffee was called "java," and music poured from the juke box. The food, unlike the food of the fifties, is healthy vegan and vegetarian. Some of the dishes are take-offs on the diner food of the fifties that tasted so good, but was so bad for you. Dishes like Fake Steak, Mock Shepherd's Pie with Salad, Southern Fried Tofu, and Apple Crumb Cake conjure up the fifties originals without inducing a coronary on the way home. This is a great place to take your non-veg. friends to coax them off meat, but it's a positive pleasure for anyone. As a chef Kate is great. She and her sister do all the healthy vegan and vegetarian. Some of the dishes are take-offs on the diner food of the fifties that tasted so good, but was so bad for you. Dishes like Fake Steak, Mock Shepherd's Pie with Salad, Southern Fried Tofu, and Apple Crumb Cake conjure up the fifties originals without inducing a coronary on the way home. This is a great place to take your non-veg. friends to coax them off meat, but it's a positive pleasure for anyone. As a chef Kate is great. She and her sister do all the cooking and baking on the premises. Their American homestyle dishes are highly original and very tasty. In keeping with the trend towards rawfood eating among vegans and vegetarians, Kate is now offering an organic living-foods menu.

KENOSHA [v]

Counter service
Midwestern American & South Indian
$5.00-9.00 (no cards)
No alcohol

543 East Twelfth Street
bet. Avenues A/ B
212-945-8053
daily 11am-11pm

Kenosha is the name of a small town in Wisconsin, which is famous for being the birthplace of the great film director and actor Orson Welles. It's also noted for being the cradle for radio announcers, who were recruited for the country's airwaves because they grew up speaking unaccented Midwestern English. So what's a nice town like Kenosha doing in a place like this? Well, one of the owners is from Kenosha, and he was nostalgic for his hometown. The other owner is Kumi Kulantri of Mumbai, the Indian restrauteur, who has had at least half a dozen restaurants--Dosaria, Thali, Tiffin, et al., shot out from under him. Together they form one of the New York restaurant scene's oddest couples. Their fare is a combination of midwestern America meets upper middle class Mumbai. We tried their Mango Soup, which is really, really good, and their Veggie Burgers, which were made with colorful shredded vegetables. Kumi made us some delicious Soy Milk Mango Lassis for dessert. We told them that to complete the decor they should put some pictures of Orson Welles on the wall.
•As of this writing, 2007, we are waiting impatiently for Kumi to open Kenosha.

LAN CAFE [ve]

Full service
Vietnamese vegan
$7.00-9.00 (no cards)
Beer & wine

342 East 6th Street
bet. 1st/ 2nd Avenue
212-228-8325
daily 11am-10pm

Last summer, we sampled vegan dishes in some Vietnamese restaurants in Hawaii--where there is a large settlement of Vietnamese folk, but, alas, no vegan Vietnamese restaurants. Admittedly, the food was very good, but the food at Lan Cafe--New York's first vegan Vietnamese restaurant-- surpasses that of the best in Honolulu. Perhaps it's because the co-owner/chef --Cao Ky and his wife Lan--are devout Mahayana Buddhists and therefore are ethical vegans. Hence, the food is 100% cruelty-free , and, on our many visits, the pure, unalloyed flavors of this essentially Buddhist Vietnamese cuisine shone forth.
   In fact, the food at Lan Cafe is so exquisite, that we played a little parlor game--we challenged each other to find a dish on the menu that we didn't like. After repeated visits, we exhausted the menu without being able to find a dish that we didn't adore. All are extraordinary. At Lan Cafe, we must speak of the extraordinary among extraordinaries. These are the best vegan eats of the East!

We recommend that you start with the classic Vietnamese dish --a staple on the menus of restaurants in Saigon--Green Papaya Salad with Mock Shrimp. Follow this with Pho--another classic Vietnamese dish. A capacious bowl is filled with a healthy serving of vegetable broth aswim with long rice noodles, and vegetarian beef. On the side are served bean sprouts and basil leaves. At intervals, these are to be added to the Pho. The flavors, of both the Green Papaya Salad and the Pho, were stupendous!

Fact is: Frank, the manager, had warned us that the Pho at Lan Cafe is so filling that there is scant room for anything else. He was right. We wanted to try the Curried Lemon Grass Seitan, and the Baguettes with Vegetarian Sausage and the one with Vegetarian Mock Ham (an incongruous Gallicism here that is doubtless the legacy of the French colonial occupation of Vietnam)--but we had to postpone those gustatory sensations for our next visit. Our only puzzlement was why was it so easy to find a table here? By rights, there should be lines of vegan gourmets winding around the block.

How did the Lan Cafe get its name. In Vietnamese the word "lan" means "orchid." "Orchidaceous" would aptly describe the cuisine--exotic, eye-filling, and drop-dead delicious!

Doug Green's LIQUITERIA [v]

Counter service
Natural organic
$3.50-5.50 (V, MC)
No alcohol

170 Second Avenue
at 11th Street
212-358-0300
Winter 7:30am-9pm
Summer 7:30am-11pm

If awards were given for the most hygienic eating establishment in town, Doug Green's Liquiteria would win it hands down. Unlike most juice bar-cum-cafes that have flyblown walls and grimy equipment, Liquiteria has gleaming tiled walls and juicers that are kept spotlessly clean. Every twenty-four hours the juicers are rotated, and disassembled, their parts bathed overnight in a biodegradable sanitizing solution. Floors and walls are scoured at the end of the day. Working surfaces are constantly being wiped down and cleaned. Fruits and vegetables are peeled and scrubbed.

Whereas most juice bars cut corners by using fruit concentrate and non-organic fruit, Doug uses only fresh ingredients and organic fruit whenever possible. And the fruit of all these labors are the most vivid-tasting, health-giving juices and smoothies in the universe. Have the Power Pina Colada Smoothie--banana strawberries, pineapple, organic apple juice. (Skip the bee pollen if you're a vegan). Or try one of Doug's Freshly-Pressed Juices. Extracted using a Norwallk hydraulic press, the most efficient juicer on the market, these juices are said to contain up to five times the minerals, vitamins and enzymes of *jus ordinaire.*

Try the Grasshopper, one of Doug's hydraulicaly-pressed green juices. It contains organic Hawaiian pineapple, organic ginger, organic wheat grass, pears, apples, and mint. Quaff it, and you'll feel like chirping with the crickets.

Heir to a vending machine business, Doug has such a passion for his work that he gave up his family business to "juice the Apple," as he phrases it. A handsome hunk of a guy, Doug--who played football two decades ago at Syracuse--is the best advertisement for the high quality of his product. (He not only owns Liquiteria but he's also its best client.)

Liquiteria enjoys the distinction of being the longest-running, free-standing juice bar in NYC. That staying power seems to have rubbed off on his workers. In an industry with high employee turnover, Doug's polite, hard-working staff have served an average of six years on the job.

Despite its name, Liquiteria doesn't reduce every solid to its liquid state. It's more than a juice bar, it's a place where one may sit down to some of the tastiest soups, salads, wraps, and sandwiches in the land. Many people start their day here with Organic Oatmeal or Organic Granola served with fresh fruit, and organic estate grown coffee. Not a few customers are so regular as to take three meals a day here.

Recently Doug hired a special chef to make vegan sushi and salads for their thriving take-out business.

Try the TLT--tempeh-bacon, red leaf lettuce, tomato and soy mayonnaise served on organic 7-grain bread. Or try that old standby, the Peanut Butter and Jelly Sandwich. Doug makes it with fresh-ground Valencia peanuts, layered with a home-made fruit spread, sliced apples and bananas. *Sacre bleu! C'est si deliceuse!*

MADRAS CAFE [v]

Full service
South Indian, kosher
$5.95-$7.95 (all major cards)
Kosher wine & beer

79 Second Avenue
bet. 4th / 5th Streets
212-254-8002
daily 12pm-3pm; 5pm-11pm

This is the only Indian restaurant in Manhattan that is truly vegan friendly. Eighty percent of the dishes on the menu are vegan, and the ones that are not are explicitly labeled "D" for dairy. The chef-owner, Sridhar Rathnam, is willing to convert any non-vegan dish on the menu to a vegan one. His is also one of the first Indian vegetarian restaurants to use TVP and other soy products in lieu of meat and dairy. Mr. Rathnam told me that he learned the recipes that he uses in the restaurant from his south Indian mother, which explains why the dishes have a down-home flavor. Unusual in an Indian eatery, the vegetables are not overly cooked and are lightly spiced. The dosas and breads are not oily, and even the deep-fried pakoras seem innocent of the oil they were cooked in. Many of our fellow diners were students and instructors from the nearby Jivamukti Yoga Center who drop in after classes. Our favorite dish was the Madras Curried Soy Chunks. But we are also partial to the Vegetable Briyani, and the Stuffed Potato Malbari (a jumbo steamed potato, stuffed with green pea masala, and simmered in traditional Kerala style coconut curry sauce). When the restaurant, Guru, closed its doors two years ago, Mr. Rathman hired one of its most talented chefs, a lady chef from Kerala. whose work in the kitchen helped elevate the level of the cuisine at Madras Cafe to stratospheric heights. For our money, it is now New York's finest Indian vegetarian restaurant.

POMMES FRITES [v]

Counter Service
Belgian French fries
$2.50-5.50 (no cards)
No alcohol

123 Second Avenue
bet. Seventh/ Eighth Streets
212-674-1234
daily 11:30am-Midnight

Studies have shown that people go to burger joints mainly for the French fries. With the opening of Pommes Frites and its opposite number, B. Frites at 1657 Broadway, it's now possible for vegetarians to dine on French Fries without having to make a clandestine visit to the Golden Arches. In Belgium, the *maison de pommes frites* is a thriving concern. So some enterprising

Americans have imported the idea to New York and judging from the lines that form up at Pommes Frites and B. Frites, it's really taking hold. The fries at Pommes Frites are double cooked in the Belgian manner, and are served with a range of tasty sauces. For vegans, it's necessary to inquire about the composition of the sauces as some may contain mayonnaise and other objectionable ingredients. We managed quite nicely with a double cone of fries that we dipped alternately in etchup and mustard, which are on the house; the other sauces are fifty cents extra.

PUKK [v] 👍

Full service
Thai vegetarian
$7.00-9.00 (all cards)
Beer, wine, champagne
www.pukknyc.com

75 First Avenue
bet. 4th/ 5th Streets
212-253-2741
daily 11:30am-11pm

A four-letter word in Thai that means "vegetable," Pukk is an apt name for this all-vegetarian Thai restaurant. Imaginatively designed to make maximum use of the rather cramped dining spaces, Pukk is a model of elegant compression. But the menu enables one to dine spaciously on delicious Thai vegetarian fare. It's not quite vegan here because, inexplicably they serve eggs?!!!? So vegans should inquire about eggs in the noodles, in the pastries, in the soups, and sauces, etc. But everything else is impeccably plant-based. In fact, the Pukksters thoughtfully provide soy milk for tea, coffee, and smoothies. For starters, try the Tom Yum Soup, a yummy soup that is aswim with chunks of spiced tofu, mushrooms, scallions and cilantro; then try the Curry Thai Pancake, a flaky crepe served in a piquant curry sauce. Follow this with the Faux Salmon; or, if you prefer to avoid faux meats, try the tofu dishes--such as Stuffed Tofu, or the Son-in-Law Tofu--at which Thai chefs excel. If there is a rawfooder in your midst, then he or she will be certain to enjoy the All Green Salad, which layers fresh vegetables on a mound of fresh greens. It is nattily and nuttily dressed with a splash of spicy peanut sauce.

Dessert here is a bit of an anticlimax after the crescendo of flavors leading up to it. So we recommend ambling over to Caravan of Dreams, or Radha for a truly scrumptious dessert.

Although the food here is not so good as that of the Thai vegan restaurant in Montreal called Chu Chai, which for our money is the best vegan restaurant in the world, it is good enough, because of its sheer exoticism, to be one of the better vegetarian restaurants in New York.

QUINTESSENCE [v] 👍

Full Service
Raw food vegetarian
$5.50-12.00 (all cards)
No alcohol
www.raw-q.com

263 East 10th Street
bet. 1st Avenue/ Avenue A
646-654-1823
daily 11:30am-11pm

For skeptics who think that raw food is a penitential diet of roots, shoots and fruits, Tolentin and her husband Dan Hoyt, who have been strict rawfoodists for four years, are on a mission to show people that rawfood can be as toothsome as it is nutritious. So admirably have they succeeded that you'd swear that some of the dishes are cooked. Ironically, the mark of a good raw food dish is that it tastes as if it's been cooked. This is certainly true of the Sun Burger, a hearty patty made of sunflower and flaxseed meal mixed with chopped celery, onions, red pepper and herbs dehydrated to a burger consistency and served between slices of dehydrated bread. {The temperature of the dehydrator in which the breads are baked must never rise above an enzyme-killing 120 degrees). Another entree, the Caribbean Nut Meatballs which are served in an aromatic, zesty pineapple-tomato sauce also earns the accolade: "Tastes as if it's been cooked." The Coconut Cream Pie and the Pecan Pie are the quintessence of desserts, fired or unfired, anywhere in the city.

WHOLE EARTH BAKERY & KITCHEN [ve]

Buffet (take-out only)
Organic vegan bakery
$,50-6.00(no cards)
No alcohol

130 St. Marks Place
bet. First Ave/Avenue A
212-677-7597
Su-Th 9am-12am
F-Sa 9am-1am

Hole-in-the-wall offering organic baked goods and small buffet, wholly vegan. The owner assures me that no honey or refined sugar is used. Cheeseless pizza, tofu-vegetable turnovers, cabbage knishes, soups and puddings along with whole-grain baked goodies of the 100% whole wheat, rather dry variety. For take-out mainly—seats four.

SOHO
(Canal Street to Houston Street)

BABYCAKES [ve] 👍

Counter service
Vegan baked goods
$1.00-4.25
www.babycakes.com

240 Broome Street
bet. Orchard/ Ludlow Streets
M-Sa 10am-10pm,
Su 10am-8pm

Although the art-deco, retro interior evokes a roadside diner from the 1920's, unless you're a dessertatarian--as we are--then it's not really possible to have a meal here; however, if you have an overdeveloped sweet tooth--as we do--then you could have a chocolate chip cookie as an appetizer, a carrot cupcake as a main course with some extra frosting on the side [It's $1.00 for a side order of frosting.]--and a slice of pound cake for dessert. You could wash it down with a cup of shade-grown, fair-trade Gorilla coffee, as we did.

Here's a rich irony--the owner, Erin McKenna, is an ovo- lacto-vegetarian, but she is scrupulous about not using eggs, or dairy. Instead of honey, she uses stevia and agave nectar --whereas, the techno-pop star Moby, who is a militant vegan, serves eggs, honey and dairy products at his restaurant, Teany, which is only a few blocks away.

Let's face it, there are a lot of excellent vegan and vegetarian restaurants in New York that have execrable desserts--Pukk, Madras Cafe, Vegetarian Dim Sum House, to list but a few. So, have your dinner at Madras Cafe; then saunter over to Babycakes for some sweet, sweet babycakes for dessert.

BLUE GREEN [ve] 👍

Counter service
Organic raw food cafe/ juice bar
$7.95-14.95 (all cards)
No alcohol.
www.bluegreenjuice.com

248 Mott Street
bet. Houston/ Prince Streets
212-334-0805
daily 9am-9pm

Compact and self-contained, like a space capsule, Blue Green is primarily a juice bar, where some of the most delicious vegan organic juice combinations and smoothies are served up. (Our favorite--the No.11: (cacao, black cherry, banana and coconut water). Blue Green is also one of chef Matthew Kenney's satellite rawfood cafes of which the Plant in Dumbo is, as it were, "the mother planet." At planet Plant, celestial rawfood eats are crafted under Kenney's supervision; then the unfired eats are shipped to each of the Blue Green Cafes. Spicy Mango Spring Roll (crispy vegetables, young coconut, green papaya, and fresh herbs), and The Torta, (which is like a squash lasagna), were our favorites, but we also enjoyed improvising our own unheated entree by purchasing a container of raw flaxseed crackers and dipping them in a Mango Salsa. We followed this with a delectable raw cheesecake, and we indulged our inner Little Jack Horner by spooning up the plump cherries at the bottom of the Black Forest Pudding.

See other locations in Brooklyn and Upper East Side.

RADHA [v]

Full Service
World vegetarian/ vegan menu
$5.95-10.95 (all cards)
Beer & wine

173 Ludlow Street
bet. Houston/ Stanton Streets
212-473-3374
Dinner Tu-Su 5pn-11pm
Brunch Sa & Su 11am-3pm

A striking holographic portrait of Radha, the consort of Lord Krishna dominates the room (a converted storefront), with its cozy booths picked out in a palette of red, gold and copper hues. Although Radha is the inspiration of this Indian-themed restaurant, its owner, Kahlil Houri, is quick to point out that the menu ventures beyond the hoary sub-continental standards of dosas, iddlys, and sabjis. He calls it "world vegetarian cuisine." Yet even the Classic Veggie Burger seems to have Indian accents and undertones. We particularly relished the Asian Temptation and the Barbecued Tofu, which were conspicuously labeled vegan, as are all the other vegan dishes on the menu. We sat under the three-dimensional portrait of Rahda. so we felt obliged to try a dish that she might have savored; we downed the vegan pakoras in her honor. The desserts, Vegan Chocolate Raspberry Cake, and Vegan Cream Cheese Truffles, were so delicious that we felt like leaving a portion of our vegan cheesecake to Radha as *prashadam* .

SULLIVAN STREET BAKERY (PIZZERIA) [v]

Counter service
Pizzeria/ baked goods
Pizzas $3.00-4.00 (all cards)
No alcohol
www.sullivanstreetbakery.com

73 Sullivan Street
bet Spring/ Broome Streets
212-334-9435
daily 7am-7pm

For lacto-vegetarians who want to go vegan, often the hardest food to give up is Pizza made with cheese. Now at last there is a place that serves vegan pizzas that are every bit as tasty as their non-vegan counterparts. One of them in particular, the Pizza Patate is so good that Martha Stewart features a recipe for it on her web site. The owner of this bakery-cum-pizzeria, Jim Lahey, actually demonstrated how to make it on Martha's TV show. It's a flat pizza topped with a layer of thinly sliced potatoes. That's how pizzas are done at Sullivan Street. Straightforward and delicious with savory toppings like the sliced Crimini mushrooms of the Pizza Funghi. Or the rosemary, olive oil and salt of the Pizza Bianca. Or the cherry tomatoes and basil of the Pizza Pugliesi. Or the tomato topping of the Pizza Pomodoro. Other pizza toppings vary with the seasons. You're allowed to sample each pizza before ordering one--which could be dangerous because you might end up ordering them all.

Located only a few blocks from the Angelika Cinema, Sullivan Street is a great place to grab a pre-cinema light supper or snack before the show. Seating is severely restricted though.

There are only two rickety chairs inside the bakery and two outside. So, if you want to sit down to enjoy your meal, take it to the Angelika cinema coffee bar and devour it there. Also, if you want condiments on your pizza, you'll have to bring your own. Sullivan Street doesn't furnish any of the extra seasonings that conventional pizza parlors do.

Vegans should watch out for the Zucchini Pizza, it's topped with appetizing Zucchini morsels, but below the top layer is a subcutaneous layer of cheese. And the Tortes are all made with butter. It pays to inquire about the ingredients before biting into anything here.

See other location at Midtown West.

TEANY [v]

Full service
International
$4.00-10.00 (all cards)
Beer & wine

90 Rivington Street
bet. Orchard/ Ludlow
212-475-9190
W, Th, Su 10am-10pm
F, Sa 10am-2am

Teany is a restaurant-cum-teahouse that was founded by the rock star Moby. Its name, Teany, stands for Tea New York, but it is also a pun, referring wryly to its diminutive size. It's teeny as well as teany.

The portions, however, are ample. For instance the *faux* turkey club sandwich, which we adored, is big enough to feed two people; and the salads, the crostini, and the granola dishes are as generous as they are delicious. Along with the Club Sandwich, we recommend the Crostini. Thin toast ovals are served with four vegan spreads--Olive, White Bean, Artichoke and Herbed Soy Cheese. It's big of Teany that after you've dipped all your toast ovals in the pots of vegan spreads, Teany will freely replenish them.

Teany desserts are tremendous! We particularly liked the Tofu Chocolate Cheese Cake, and the Peanut Butter Chocolate cake, which are supplied to Teany by the Vegan Treats bakery.

The eponymous tea menu is as extensive as any four star restaurant's wine list. Last time we were there, we savored the black tea called Golden Monkey,. but there are uncaffeinated herb teas as well. Sad to report: we found the homemade sodas to be flavorless and insipid.

Although Moby is co-owner of the restaurant with his ex-girlfriend Kelly Tisdale, he likens himself to a Victorian father who sees the baby only now and then. He writes the checks but Kelly does the day-to-day running of the shop. In providing such delicious fare in such a tastefully designed space, however teeny--Moby has done the community a whale of a service. Incidentally, Moby, (nee Richard Melvile Hall), is nicknamed after the whale in his distant ancestor, Herman Melvile's novel *Moby Dick*. He is a committed vegan; one could only wish that he had extended his veganism to the entire menu. Vegan dishes are marked with an asterisk.

TIEN GARDEN [ve]

Full service
Chinese Homestyle
$5.95-8.75 (all cards)
No alcohol

170 Allen Street
at E. Houston/ 1st Avenue
212-388-1364
M-Sa 12pm-10pm

Not so long ago, Tiengarden was a lonely outpost of veganism on the lower East Side. Now it may be seen as something of a neighborhood trendsetter. Within the past two years it has become surrounded by eco-conscious stores like Earth Matters and Bluestockings; tony vegan boutiques like MooShoes, and Organic Avenue; and fashionable vegetarian restaurants like Teany.

Based on the ancient theory of five elements--metal, water, earth, metal, and fire--the food at Tiengarden is prepared in such a way as to maximize its *chi*, or life force. On the other hand, foods that are considered to be sapping of one's *chi* are scrupulously avoided. So in addition to being vegan, (because animal products are considered to be deleterious to one's *chi*); the dishes contain no garlic, or onions, which are also held to be harmful to one's *chi*. Nonetheless, the food is quite delectable without these flavor intensifiers.

We are partial to their Pan-Fried Bean Curd Sandwich, their Mixed Gluten Salad (Spicy braised wheat gluten is served on a bed of lettuce with tomato, celery and carrot sticks and served with a vegan barbecue sauce or vegan mayo.); their Special Nuggets (soy nuggets, red bell peppers, broccoli, cauliflower, zucchini, cashews in a light curry peanut sauce). We also ate with gusto their Basil Beancurd (crisp, layered beancurd with broccoli, tomato and mushrooms in basil sauce).

Unlike most Chinese restaurants, desserts here are totally vegan, substantial, and delicious--and, like the rest of the food, even their home-made fresh pies and cakes are *chi*-enhancing.

WILD GINGER [v] 👍

Full service
Pan-Asian
$10.00-13.00 (all cards)
Beer, wine & sake
www. wildgingernyc.com

380 Broome Street
bet. Mott/ Mulberry Streets
212-966-1883/ 2669
Daily 12pm-11pm

Three friends--Richard, (the architect and co-manager), Winnie (the accountant and manager), and her husband, Tim (the chef)--have pooled their assets, as it were, to create one of the most popular and successful vegetarian restaurants in town. Richard is responsible for the elegant yet cozy interior; Winnie, for the crisply efficient running of the place; and Tim for the tasty dishes. "Pan Asian" is how they describe their cuisine--Thai, Chinese, Malaysian and Indian--and for once the menu truly deserves this overused and often inaccurate appellation.

We practically shouted our adulation of the Scallion Pancakes with the Home-Made Mango Salsa, which tasted less like crepes than small pizzas topped with a piquant mango sauce. We adored the Samosa in Curry Sauce. For the main course, our taste buds thrilled to the exotic flavor notes in Malaysian Curry Stew (Mild, Slow-Cooked Coconut Curry with Soy Protein, Broccoli, Carrots, Potatoes and Pumpkin). and Mango Soy Protein (Thin-Slice Medallions Sautéed in a Mellow Plum Sauce with Mango, Zucchini, Sweet-Sage Turnips, Peppers, and Onions).

Beverages--we tossed off the homemade Wild Ginger Beer, and Virgin Mojitoes with gusto. They were--at least to our teetotal, non-alcoholic sensibilities-- bewitching. For drinkers of more adult beverages, there is an array of beers, wine and sakes that are guaranteed to "bewitch, bother and bewilder." Vegans, however, should beware the Lassis (an Indian drink made with fruit juice and yogurt). Order soy-milk Lassis instead!

Chef Tim accrued his repertoire of Pan-Asian vegan dishes by working in a string of different veg. restaurants--such as Zen Palate, Tien Garden and assorted others--as a sous-chef. But by now, Tim has clearly outstripped his masters; so while one may recognize many of the menu dishes from having dined elsewhere, seldom have they been prepared to such palate-pleasing perfection.

Notes

BELOW CANAL STREET
(Includes Chinatown, Tribeca, Financial District)

BUDDHA BODAI VEGETARIAN RESTAURANT [v]

Full service
Chinese (kosher)
$7.95-14.95 (all cards)
No alcohol.

5 Mott Street
at Bowery
212-566-8388
daily 10:30am-10:30pm

See description under Queens

HOUSE OF VEGETARIAN [v]

Full service
Chinese vegetarian
$4.50-10.95 (no cards)
Beer & wine

68 Mott Street
bet. Canal/Bayard Streets
212-226-6572
daily 11am-11pm

This is one Chinatown restaurant where there aren't any fresh kills hanging in the window. "All We Are Served Vegetarian Dishes" reads the reassuring note on the extensive menu of more than 200 dishes, from Vegetarian Roast Duck (too much of a poultry flavor for our taste) to Braised Chicken with Lily Flowers (made from wheat gluten) or everybody's favorite, Iron Steak, made from yams and quite tasty. Our own personal favorite were mock Chicken with Mango and Black Mushrooms With Soysticks. Served in a narrow dining room with plastic tablecloths and no ambiance, but the food's good and there's plenty of it.

VEGETARIAN DIM SUM HOUSE [ve]

Full service
Chinese
$4.95-12.95 (no cards)
No alcohol

24 Pell Street
at Mott Street
212-577-7176
daily 11am-11pm

Vegetarian Dim Sum House serves most of the same dishes that its sister restaurant, House of Vegetarian, serves except that it offers them amid posher surroundings with a wider range of dim sum dishes. "Dim Sum" (literally "cooked snacks") are the snack-like dishes that are popular in Hong Kong, Taiwan and other parts of South China. The Cantonese like to put together several dim sum dishes for breakfast, lunch and tea; they even have a few dim sum dishes as appetizers before dinner. Because they may eat dim sum three or four times a day, these snacks have to be skillfully prepared to avoid boring the jaded palate. The dim sum that we had at the Dim Sum House were certainly unboring. We particularly liked the Spinach Dumpling, the Lotus Root Cake, and the Sticky Rice wrapped in Lotus Leaf. From the main course menu, we liked the mock roast duck and the mock chicken dishes made from tofu skin. Portions are generous and service is attentive.

BOOKS BY RYNN BERRY

FAMOUS VEGETARIANS
and their favorite recipes

Lives and Lore from Buddha to the Beatles

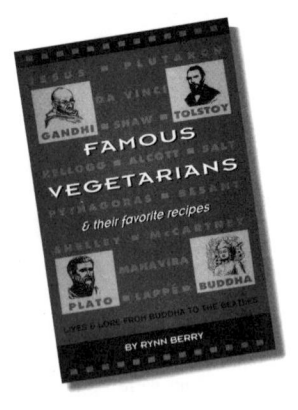

"Berry writes beautifully, with a genuine gustatory relish for words and savory asides. The recipes are delightful...many researched and translated for the first time." — *The Boston Book Review*

"Scholarship at the end of a fork — and for writing it Berry deserves an 'A'."
— *Vegetarian Times*

"Entertaining and educational..."
— *Vegetarian Voice*

"Impeccably researched and written."
— *The Animals' Agenda*

"The 70 recipes are not only fascinating, but have been kitchen-tested by the author for savoriness..." — *Yoga Journal*

292 pages   **$15.95** *paperback*

Copy this form to order books. Other books by Rynn Berry on reverse side.

PYTHAGOREAN PUBLISHERS / P.O. Box 8174 / New York, NY 10116

____ copies *Famous Vegetarians & Their Favorite Recipes* @ $15.95	$ _____
____ copies *The New Vegetarians* @ $10.95	$ _____
____ copies *Food for the Gods* @ $19.95	$ _____
Add postage: $3.00 for one book, $1.00 for each additional book	$ _____
TOTAL ENCLOSED	$ _____

NAME _____

ADDRESS _____

CITY _____ STATE/ZIP _____ PHONE _____

GO VEGAN
for the animals, the planet, & optimal health

Vegan Lifestyle Coach
Andrew Glick
Certified Holistic Health Counselor
845-679-7979

andy@meatfreezone.org
www.meatfreezone.org
Complimentary Initial Phone Consultation

FREE DELIVERY ($10 min)   CLOSED ON MONDAYS

100% VEGAN

spot

156 5th Ave. (Btwn Douglass & Degraw)
Park Slope, Brooklyn
718.622.2275 • thevspotcafe.com

Latin, Italian & American cuisine   We also carry Vegan Treats

---

NOW IN TWO LOCATIONS

Candle 79 154 East 79th Street (bet. Lex & 3rd)
ph.212.537.7179

Candle Cafe 1307 Third Avenue at 75th Street
ph.212.472.0970; fx.212.472.7169

The Candle Cafe Cookbook is now available
at the restaurant, your local bookstore, & amazon.com

Voted Vegetarian Restaurant of the Year
Time Out New York, 2006
www. candlecafe. com

BROOKLYN

BLUE GREEN [ve]

Counter service
Organic raw food cafe/ juice bar
$7.95-14.95 (all cards)
No alcohol.
www.bluegreenjuice.com

25 Jay Street (DUMBO)
bet. John/ Plymouth Streets
718-722-7541
daily 9am-6pm

See description under Upper East Side
See other locations in Upper East Side and Soho

BLISS [v]

Full service
Natural
$2.50-6.00 (no cards)
No alcohol

191 Bedford Avenue
bet. N6th / N7th Streets
718-599-2547
daily 8am-11pm

"Bliss was it in that dawn to be alive and eating brunch at Bliss, but to be vegetarian was very heaven!" is what Wordsworth might have written had he been a vegetarian and had he had the good fortune to dine at Bliss--one of New York's best vegetarian restaurants. He would surely have waxed poetic over the vegan BLT's that are made with Fakin' Bacon, the Veggie Burgers and the Seitan "Steak" Sandwiches. The salads are a tone poem and the desserts an ode to Bliss. With prices so much lower in Williamsburg than for comparable fare in Manhattan, it's worth hopping the L train and traveling East just one stop from Manhattan for so much more bliss for the buck.
• Recent visits, in early 2007, yielded less bliss for the buck, but it's still worth s subway jaunt.

BODY AND SOUL[ve]

Food stand
International, organic
$4.00-6.00 (no cards)
No alcohol

Farmers' Market
at Grand Army Plaza
212-982-5870
Sa 8am-4pm
Sa 8am-4pm

One of the best ways to keep body and soul together in the city is to have a light vegan meal at the vegan food stand in the Grand Army Plaza Farmers' market., which is called aptly enough Body and Soul. Started by the owners of Counter restaurant back in 1994, it draws throngs of hungry folk for breakfast, lunch, early light suppers, and snacks. And it's easy to see why. The out-size wraps and turnovers are scrumptious. Try the Saffron Potato wrap which teases the palate with plantain chunks hidden inside. Or try the Spinach Portabello Turnover, which is filled with tofu ricotta, and tastes a bit like a Spinach Lasagna. You might want to complement this with a dairy-free Blueberry Muffin, Or a Sweet Potato Muffin. Don't leave the stand without biting into a melt-in-your-mouth Chocolate Brownie, or a Wheat-Free Almond Cookie. Then repair to one of the benches in Prospect Park and have an *al fresco* meal.

CAFE KAI [v]

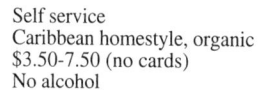

Self service
Caribbean homestyle, organic
$3.50-7.50 (no cards)
No alcohol

151 Smith Street
bet. Bergen/ Wycoff Streets
718-596-3466
M-F 8am-7pm,
Sa 10:30 am-7:30pm
Su 11am-5pm

As mentioned in a our review of Goga Cafe; the restaurant scene in South Brooklyn is making a comeback after the recent demise of five vegetarian/vegan restaurants within about six months of each other. And Cafe Kai is definitely a herald of that comeback Although Cafe Kai bills itself as "a juice bar with a twist," to call it a mere juice bar is to do it an injustice. Cafe Kai serves first rate vegan food, ninety percent of which is organic. We commend to your palates the following items: the Hickory Smoked Tempeh Sandwich, the Tex-Mex, a sandwich consisting of roasted pepper, tomato, cilantro, soy jalapeno cheese on a whole grain baguette. For entrees, we liked Curried Chick Peas with Mango and the Thai Style Stewed Eggplant--eggplant, tempeh, coconut milk, rosemary. For dessert try the Mango Upside Down Cake, which is made by the proprietor, Lisa De Leon's mother. And don't forget to wet your whistle with a Cafe Kai beverage. It is, after all, a juice bar with a twist. We recommend the Peanut Punch, a shake containing soy ice-cream, soy milk, protein powder. Or a Rainforest Fruit Smoothie, containing acai, apple juice, strawberry and banana. If you're still hungry have a Vegan Muffin, or a slice of Sweet Potato Bread. Kai is the West African Yoruba word for lovable and the food at Cafe Kai is nothing if not lovable.

"D" ITAL SHAK [ve]

Counter service
Trinidadian vegan (no cards)
$5.00-8.00
No alcohol

989 Nostrand Aveune
bet. Empire / Sullivan
718-756-6557
M-Sa 24 hours

According to the Trinidadian family who runs this highly successful vegan eatery, in Trinidadian patois, "D" stands for the article "the." The word "Ital" in Caribbean creole means vegan. The unique feature of this restaurant, which sets it apart from every other vegan establishment in New York City, is that it is open 24 hours a day. So, if you're a Manhattanite and are suddenly seized with a craving for Ackee Patties or Callaloo at two in the morning, then jump on the number two train and get thee to "D" Ital Shak. The most popular dish on the menu is a vegetarian version of macaroni and cheese, which is made with soy cheese. The Sorrel and Mauby drinks are bracing, and the dessert, Plantain Tart, is as sinful as it sounds. The place is always packed, even at two in the morning. (It's so successful, in fact, that the managers said that they didn't need to be mentioned in the *Vegan Guide!*) So be prepared to stand in line. Your taste buds will thank you.

FOODSWINGS [ve] 👍

Counter service
Fast food
$4.25-6.95 (all cards)
No alcohol

295 Grand Street
bet. Roebling/ Havemeyer
718-388-1919
T-Th 2pm-11pm;
F 2pm-2am, Sa 12pm-2am;
Su 11am-11pm

The most conscientious fast-food joint on the planet, this has got to be. The owner, Freedom Tripodi, is on a mission to stamp out the addictive, carnivorous fastfoodism that is rampaging through the nation. He is fighting it by providing a tasty range of vegan fast food edibles that surpass even those served at Red Bamboo and Kate's Joint. What's his secret? Perhaps it's that he's added to his food a subtle ingredient--a dash of compassion. For instance, he is emphatic about serving food that is free of dairy products and honey; he donates his food and his services to animal rights organizations. (Recently he catered a Farm Sanctuary Gala *gratis*.) And, he puts out vegan munchies after 11pm so that the clients of the numerous taverns in the neighborhood will have vegan treats to snack on when they stagger through the door for a postprandial feed.

They're all here--vegan versions of the abominable but addictive foods concocted by Colonel Sizzle-Hop MacWendys. Fish sticks, chicken nuggets, hot dogs, fried shrimp, buffalo wings, hamburgers, cheese burgers, drumsticks, et al. By far the most popular dish (according to Freedom) is the Faux Philly Cheese Steak Sandwich, but we preferred the mock No Chicken Parmigiana Sandwich.(breaded chicken cutlets, with soy mozzarella covered in tomato sauce, served on warm Italian bread), and the No Turkey Club, (a double decker sandwich with pepper soy turkey slices, crispy soy bacon, romaine lettuce and tomato) is better than Teany's. It comes with your choice of soy mayo or mustard. We also liked the Foodswings Pu-Pu Platter, which contains 2 Mock Nuggets, 2 Sea Styx, 2 "Shrimp," and 1 each of Foodwings Drumsticks, as well as the sauces that come with each--such as Bleu Cheese, Agave-Mustard, Tartar, BBQ--that are mocked to a fare thee well.

Best of all, are the French Fries, (Freedom Fries?), which put those served by the Golden Arches to shame. [Studies have shown that people go to the Golden Arches and other burger joints mainly for the French Fries.]

Prepared off premises by two companies, Vegan Treats and Miss Vegan Goddess, the desserts here are otherworldly. We especially liked the faux cheesecake, and the Strawberry Cake, but our favorite, was the Key-Lime Pie created by Sarah Sohn, "Miss Vegan Goddess." Eat the food here and you'll feel like a vegan god or goddess just out of your teens.

4 COURSE VEGAN [ve] 👍

Full service
International, organic
$40.00 prix-fixe (no cards)
Organic wine
www.4 course vegan.com

Williamsburg Loft
(Call for precise location)
718-599-5913
Sa/ Su 7-11pm

Just ten blocks away from the restaurant Bliss, an even more blissful dining experience awaits you. In a Williamsburg loft, two idealistic ethical vegans, Matteo Silverman and Gregory Bodock have created an offbeat culinary experience that every New Yorker, veg or non-veg, owes it to his taste buds to partake of. Fast friends since they worked together at Green's, a renowned vegetarian restaurant in San Francisco, Greg and Matteo decide what dishes they're going to feature for the following Sunday, then post them on their website--www.4coursevegan.com. They also send out hard copies of the bill of fare to stores like Moo Shoes, where we first learned about them. The menu changes weekly, and one must call or Email to make reservations, and to ask for directions on how to find their loft..

On the night we visited, there were twelve guests, among whom two were vegans, three were ovo-lacto vegetarians, the rest were carnivores. Which made for a lively evening. We sat next to a Belgian artist, a denizen of Williamsburg, whose favorite dish in the world was *viand du cheval,* a delicacy in Belgium. They even have restaurants dedicated to that detestable dish. So we had a heated discussion on the merits of veganism vs. the demerits of *viand du cheval.*

That's the great thing about Four Course Vegan. It's a sort of vegan "My Dinner With Andre." But playing verbal tennis with our table mates did not prevent us from savoring each course. We started with Meyer Lemon Aleppo Chile Aioli. This was followed by Creamy Artichoke and Baby Spinach Phyllo Triangles. Then for the *piece de la resistance,* we were served Spring Vegetable Paella with Spiced Seitan Smoked Tofu, and Saffron Basmati Rice. Dessert was Pecan Tart with Vanilla Bean Ice Cream and Chocolate Chards. It's refreshing to dine out and not have to ask if there's any milk in the soup, casein in the dip, or honey in the dessert. Chef Matteo is such a principled vegan that he won't have these "ingredients" in his kitchen.

FOUR SEASONS RESTAURANT [ve}

Counter service
Caribbean vegetarian
$4.00-10.00 {no cards}
No alcohol

2281 Church Avenue
at Bedford Avenue
718-693-7996
M-Th 9am-10pm
Fr-Sa 9am-12; Su 11am-7pm

This is not to be confused with the higher rent, higher cholesterol restaurant of the same name in Manhattan. This is the healthier vegetarian version. It's Fresh Assorted Curries, Vegetarian Lo Mein, Vegan Baked Goods and Fresh-Squeezed Juices will delight your palate and are guaranteed to ward off a thrombosis.

THE GREENS [ve]

Full service
Vegan Kosher Chinese
$5.25--9.50 (M,V)
No alcohol

128 Montague Street. 1 Fl
at Henry Street
718-246-1288
Su-Th 11:30am-10:30pm
F-Sa 12noon-11pm

If you've ever dined at Zen Palate and wished that the portions could be cheaper and more plentiful then you should bring your appetite to the Greens. Here all your dishes will be fulfilled. Dishes are of Zen-Palate quality or better at Chinatown prices or cheaper. The head chef, Long Huei Su, earned his stripes by cooking in the vegetarian kitchens of Taiwan. Start with a delicately flavored Wanton Soup and Steamed Spinach Dumplings. For a main course, have the Festival in the Roll, which consists of a crisp tofu crepe stuffed with lightly cooked vegetables--string beans, carrots, beans sprouts, black mushrooms, celery, served with a spicy dipping sauce. On the side, have a serving of lightly fried rice, mixed with wilted spinach and soy protein. Thick rice noodles are another unusual side dish. The great thing about the Greens is that you could order a meal by tossing a chopsticks at the menu, and each time you'd hit the mark.

IMHOTEPS [ve]

Self service
West Indian vegetarian, organic
$5-10 (no cards)
No alcohol

734 Nostrand Ave.
bet. Park Place & Prospect
718-493-2395
daily- 8:30am-12am

Imhoteps is the name of an Egyptian minister during the reign of the pharaoh Zoser, who ruled Egypt about 2650 BCE. Imhotep's wisdom was so vast that he has been deified as the creator of medicine and the epitome of sagacity. The owners of this Brooklyn eatery--Tonde and Maketa--named both their first son and their restaurant after this legendary Egyptian sage. Had Imhoteps been a chef then he could not have crafted a tastier or a healthier cuisine than the food that is on offer at Imhoteps. The chef Victor Telesford was the founding chef at Veggie Castle, and his skill at the stove did a lot to make Veggie Castle the roaring success that it is today. The food is so seductive that many customers eat three meals a day here. Among the dishes that are especially recommended are Soy Salmon and Vegie Roast Duck, but everything on the menu is mouth-watering. The beverages, which include protein shakes, sorrel, wheat grass and sea-moss juices are healthful and bracing. We had a glass of Sorrel with our Soy Salmon and Veggie Roast Duck and topped off our meal with a Carrot Sea Moss vegan ice cream that was laced with gingko--the memory enhancing herb--that made the whole culinary experience even more unforgettable.

NATURAL MYSTIC [ve]

Counter service
Trinidadian vegan
$3.00-6.00 (no cards)
No alcohol

740 Nostrand Avenue
bet. Sterling/ Park Place
718-953-4560
daily 8am-11:30pm

Mr. Chococop is the quaint name of the rasta chef who presides over this Ital eatery. He serves up delicious vegan food with a Trinidadian island spin--Barbecue Soya Chunks. Soya Fish, Soya Ribs, Mango Chow, Ackee with Soya. Wash everything down with a schooner of sugarcane juice. His dishes compare favorably with those of the other Ital food emporia on Nostrand Avenue, which is saying a lot.

RAS DIGGI [ve]

Full service
Ital food
$5.00-7.00 (no cards)
No alcohol

819 Park Place
bet. Nostrand/ Rogers Avenues
718-604-8585
daily 11am-12am

If you dig Rastafarian or "Ital" food, as we do, then you've come to the right place. We had Long

Green Beans with Tofu, and Black-Eyed Peas served with "bake"(fried dumplings).The look of the place, which is an unprepossessing storefront, belies the quality of the tasty vegan dishes that the Rasta chef dishes up here. One note of caution. Theoretically the restaurant is open everyday from 11am to midnight, but the place closes as soon as the daily batch of food sells out, which frequently happens by 2pm..

RED BAMBOO [v] 👍

Full service
Asian soul food fusion
$9.95-12.95 (all cards)
No alcohol
www.redbamboobrooklyn.com

271 Adelphi Street
at DeKalb Avenue
718-643-4352
Tu-F 12pm-12am
Sa-Su 11am-12am

See description under Greenwich Village

STRICTLY VEGETARIAN [ve]

Counter service
Carribean vegetarian
$4.00-8.00 (no cards)
No alcohol

2268 Church Avenue
bet.Bedford/Flatbush Avenues
718-284-2543
daily noon-11:30pm

Just down the street from Veggie Castle with which it can bear comparison, this place serves such delicious Carribean vegetarian dishes as Chick Pea Stew, Vegetable Chow Mein and Tofu Stew. The menu changes daily.

TCHEFA [v]

Self service
Carribean vegetarian
$6-10 (all cards)
No alcohol

512 Flatbush Avenue
bet. Lefferts Ave/ Empire Blvd.
718-284-6742
M-F 4pm-9pm
Sa-Su 12pm-10pm

According to Queen Mother Maast Amm Amen, the Bronx-born boss and chef of Tchefa, in ancient Egyptian "Tchefa" means "divine foods." Which is certainly an apt description of the foods on offer at Tchefa. Every morsel that we sampled was divine! Maast learned the knack of infusing her food with divine flavor during a twenty-year stint as a cook for the local Ausen Auset church, an African-based church most of whose members are vegans!
    A striking-looking lady, who proudly proclaims her age to be 58, Maast doesn't look a day over 35--ample testimony to the rejuvenative powers of her divine cuisine. We downed the Sesame Medallion Bean Curd Duck, and Escoviche Soy Fish with a side order of Mixed Veggies and Macaroni and Soy Cheese. For dessert, we scoffed her carrot cake and chased it with a Raspberry-Strawberry Smoothie. Maast told us that the staff of the Brooklyn Botanical Garden, whose entrance is only a flowerpot's throw from the restaurant, often repair to Tchefa for meals. Ditto for the staff of the Brooklyn Museum. Fact is: it's a great place to chow down after you've toured either the Brooklyn Muesum or the Brooklyn Botanical Gardens.
    •One important caveat: The Tchefa staff often go on long religious retreats. In their absence, the restaurant is shuttered and their phone rings incessantly. (It's not hooked up to an

answering machine;) so it's easy to get the impression that they're out of business. We inadvertently de-listed them from the guide last year because, they were on an extended religious retreat when we came a-calling.

THE V-SPOT [ve] 👍

Full service
South American/ Italian vegan
$5.00-10.00 (all cards)
Beer & wine
thevspotcafe.com

156 Fifth Avenue
bet. Douglass/ Degraw Streets
718-622-2275
T-Th 11am -10:pm
F-Su 11am-11pm
Brunch Sa-Su 11am-4pm

Verily an erogenous zone for the vegan palate is Dan Caberno's new Park Slope vegan eatery called the "V-spot." Here the dishes are. in the uncensored words of a lady friend, who dines there often--"Sooooo goooood!" We certainly wanted to have what she was having; so we ventured over to the V-Spot to see what all the fuss and bother was about. There in an intimate room, with black-and-white photos of Brooklyn adorning exposed brick walls, we savored the V-Spot experience.
    Serious vegans, will be impressed by the V-Spot's dedication to ethical standards. The menu proclaims: "All of our dishes are strictly vegetarian.That is, they do not contain any meat chicken, fish, eggs, milk, cheese, honey, casein, gelatin, whey or any other animal or animal derived product. Our mock meat products contain meat and soy." Clearly the V in this V-Spot is not for Vengeance, but for Victory!
    Dan, the owner, who often doubles as a waiter, took our order. A high-school math-teacher-turned-vegan restaurateur, Dan is a true Pythagorean.{Pythagoras,--as you were probably not instructed in your high school geometry classes--founded a society for the study of mathematics in ancient Greece which required that its initiates be strict vegetarians or vegans.]
    Most of the dishes on the menu are based on family recipes--such as the appetizer Empanadas--that Dan inherited from his Colombian mother and grandmother. Even the seemingly prosaic Steak with Rice & Beans--is reminiscent of the authentic *comida* to be had in the village *cantinas* of South America. Its authenticity--albeit veganized,--is why it, and so many of the other dishes with a Latin flair, are so utterly transporting.
    The Latin flair extends to Italian specialties such as Penne with Vodka Sauce, Rigatoni with Eggplant; Meatball Parmigiana Hero, the Bean Burger and the Pizza Burger that danced fandangos on our tongue. Piquant also were the side orders of Spinach with Garlic and Oil; Yucca; Sweet Potato Fries, and Quinoa with Mixed Vegetables and Kale. Desserts are the dependably scrumptious vegan treats from Vegan Treats Bakery.

👍 Indicates we especially recommend this restaurant for the quality of the food.

VEGETARIAN PALATE

Full service
Chinese
$5.95-10.95 (all cards)
No alcohol

258 Flatbush Avenue
Bet Prospect Park/ St. Marks
781 623-8809
M-Th 11:30am-11pm
Fr, Sa 11:30am,-12:00am
Su: 12:00--11:00pm

Vegetarian Palate probably has the most extensive menu of any vegetarian restaurant in the city. Which reminds us of the famous adage that one should never play cards with someone named " Doc," or eat in a restaurant named "Mom's,"--or in one that has a superabundance of items on the menu. Like most Chinese vegan restaurants Vegetarian Palate abounds in mock meats--as witness their vegetarian seafood dish, Ocean Harvest, which features a collection of vegetarian shrimp, scallops, and squid served with broccoli, snow peas, and baby corn. But the ultimate mock meat *tour de force* is their Paella Valencia , which is composed of sundry mock seafoods such as shrimp, scallops, crab, mock chicken, mock eel, tofu, shitake mushrooms with mixed vegetables. The service is crisply efficient, the decor, garish. Other diners have complained of excessive starch and oil in the dishes, but one may request of the waiter that these additives be omitted. We had the Soy Chicken with Spinach in Curry Sauce, and the Soy Lemon Chicken and our palates were beguiled by them. For dessert we indulged ourselves in a Banana Split, made with three scoops of non-dairy ice-cream covered with sprinkles and chocolate syrup--all of which soothed our vegetarian palate.

VEGGIE CASTLE [v]

Counter service
Caribbean vegetarian
$2.50-7.50 (all major cards)
No alcohol

2242 Church Avenue
bet. Flatbush/Bedford Avenues
719-703-1275
Su-Tu 8am-11pm; F-Sa 8am-12am

The farm animals have revolted and taken over the farm? The hostages have overpowered their captors? The oppressed have overthrown their oppressors? And the vegetarians have taken over a fast food restaurant? These are wishful headlines that we would like to read in tomorrow's newspaper, but in the case of Veggie Castle the wishful headline has already come true. Some enterprising vegetarian business folks have taken over a former burger joint and turned it into a vegetarian restaurant that serves the Veggie Castle Burger along with an array of delicious dishes that you won't find in your typical fast food place --such as Curried Soy Chicken, BBQ Soy Chunks With Pineapple, and ersatz Shepherd's Pie. I had a Spicy Black Bean Burger that was much the best veggie burger I'd ever tasted. I followed this with an order of Turmeric Bean Curd Duck that really showed off to advantage the culinary talent of the chefs at Veggie Castle. Instead of soda pop and shakes, Veggie Castle's juice bar serves a range of fresh fruit/vegetable juices and Smoothies .Veggie Castle is giving fast food such a good name that, in the future, burger joints may soon be dishing up Wheat Grass Juice and Veggie Burgers. It's cause for hope.

QUEENS

ANNAM BRAHMA [v]

Full service
Indian vegetarian
$4.00-12.00 (all cards)
No alcohol

84-43 164th Street
at Hillside Avenue
718-523-2600
M-Tu,Th-Sa 11am-10pm
W 11am-4pm; Su 12-10pm

This year marks the thirty-sixth anniversary of Annam Brahma, making it one of the most venerable vegetarian restaurants in the city. It was started and is currently operated by followers of the spiritual leader Sri Chimnoy, who encourages his pupils to observe a vegetarian diet, to meditate and to give something back to the community. (Pictures of Chimnoy running marathons and striking poses festoon the walls). His pupils founded this restaurant to contribute to the common weal; and the high quality of the food bespeaks their dedication to higher principles. Particularly recommended are the delicious Chapati Roll-Ups that are stuffed with either an American Veggie Burger filling or an Indian Curry filling, and the Veggie Kebabs made with soy meat.

BOMBAY SIZZLERS [v]

Full service
Indian
$7.95-14.95 (all cards)
No alcohol.

24803 Union Turnpike,
(Bellrose)
718-343-8499
M-Th 12am-4pm; 6pm-11pm
F 12pm-4pm; 6pm-11pm
Sa 12pm-4pm; 6pm-11pm
Su 10am-4pm; 6pm-10

This is a vegetarian parody of the fast food restaurant chain that is better known for its sizzle than its sustenance. Quite the opposite is true of the food served at Bombay Sizzlers. Every dish that we sampled not only sizzled, but it sparkled with the spicy piquancy of the finest Indian cuisine. We came for the lunch buffet--which at $5.95 is a bargain--and marveled at the array of *dal* (bean) dishes that lay before us in a profusion of colors. The regular menu features a number of unique items that entice the adventurous palate. For instance, they feature a line of dishes called "Sizzlers" that are a take-off on other cuisines, including Indian style Italian and Mexican food. Recommended for vegans are the Vegetable Jalfrezzi, the Channa Masala, and the Alu Gobi. But the chefs stand ready to make any lacto-veg. dish to vegan standards. For our dessert, the chefs were able to scrounge some dates rolled in shredded coconut. But if you're seeking a more elaborate confection you won't be able to find it here. Despite the lack of dessert choices for vegans, all in all, we feel it's definitely worth the hour and twenty minutes by train and bus that it takes to commute here. From 42nd Street, take the F train to Kew Gardens. Then hop on the Q46 bus and alight at 248th Street.

BUDDHA BODAI [v]

Full service
Chinese (kosher)
$7.95-14.95 (all cards)
No alcohol.

42-96 Main Street
at Cherry Avenue
718-939-1188
daily 11am-11pm

There is a wide array of dishes to choose from--Veg. Snail to Sweet and Sour Fish. Indeed, the range of ersatz is so exhaustive that it put us in mind of those Taoist temple kitchens in which chefs flaunt their ingenuity by creating ever more elaborate mock meat dishes. But we did not enjoy our dining experience here; mainly because the manager was brusque and discourteous and refused to entertain any questions as to which dishes were vegan and which were not.

DIMPLE INDIAN FAST FOOD [v]

Counter service
Indian Vegetarian

35-68 73rd Street
at 37th Avenue
718-458-8144

For description and hours, see the Manhattan listing under Midtown East.

DOSA DINER [v]

Full service
South Indian
$4-5 (no cards)
No alcohol

35-66 73rd Street
at 37th Avenue
718-205-2218
11:30am-10pm

"Nothing could be finer than dosas from this diner" is a ditty that one might recite after eating the dosas here. We highly recommend the Vegetable Dosa and the Vegetables Uthappam. In Jackson Heights, the uthappams and the dosas are bigger, the fillings more generous, and the food spicier, but also more dairy-laden than in Manhattan. The saving grace is that the prices are much more reasonable out here than in the Big Dosa.

DOSA HUTT [v]

Counter service
South Indian Vegetarian
$3.00-8.00 (no cards)

45-63 Bowne Street
(Flushing)
718-961-5897
daily 10am-9pm

No alcohol

This is India's answer to the Pizza Hut. Dosas, which are enormous crepes filled with spicy potato mixtures, do bear a resemblance to pizza, but I'll take a dosa over a pizza any time. The dosas here are tip-top, We especially relished the Masala Dosa. As with Dossa Diner, they're biigger and cheaper here than in the Big Dosa!

HAPPY BUDDHA [ve]

Full service
Chinese
$4.00-10.00 (major cards)
No alcohol
www.happybuddha.com

135-37 37th Avenue
(Flushing)
718-358-0079
daily 11am-10pm

There are a myriad of tasty dishes on the menu that would make the Buddha and any other vegetarian very happy indeed. The Vegetarian Mock Duck was a personal favorite.

HEALTH CONSCIOUS NATURAL FOODS [ve]

Buffet, counter service
Caribbean, organic
$4.00-6.00 (all cards)
No alcohol

231-22 Merrick Boulevard
(Laurelton)
718-712-7740
W-Sa 9:30am-8pm
Su-Tu 9:30am-7pm

Larry, the owner of this health food market-cum-restaurant, serves delicious Caribbean style vegan cuisine. He makes a lip-smacking Ital Stew, which contain peas, carrots, coconut milk, etc. Fresh soup is prepared every day. as are such Caribbean staples as Baked Plantain, Ackee, Organic Peas and Brown Rice, Freshly Prepared Kale and Collard Greens, and Sweet Potato Pudding. Larry and his wife give even American dishes like Veggie Burgers, Veggie Meatloaf a creative fillip that keeps customers coming back for more-- from the tri-state area, and all five boroughs.

LINDA'S ORGANIC KITCHEN AND MARKET [ve]

Buffet./counter service
International, American
$3.00-6.00 (all cards)
No alcohol

81-22 Lefferts Boulevard
bet. Austin Street//83rd Avenue
212-847-2233
M-F 10am-7pm
Sa 10am-6pm; Su 11am-5:30pm

While you're shopping at Linda's Organic Market, in the tree-fringed streets of Kew Gardens, it's nice to know that you can grab a quick bite just a few steps away at Linda's Organic Kitchen. Like Integral Yoga, Linda's has a vegetarian deli and juice bar where you may indulge your appetite without compromising your karma. The vegan desserts are baked daily. Linda, who grew up in Hawaii, exudes good health, and has a sunny personality. She, herself, prepares all the yummy dishes--from casseroles to sandwiches, to fruit pies. If you're a salad lover, you're in luck. Linda prepares composed salads such as Quinoa Salad, Artichoke Salad, and Vegan Sushi

MAHARAJAH QUALITY [v]
SWEETS & SNACKS

Full service
International vegetarian
$400-12.00 (all cards)
No alcohol

73-10 37th Avenue
bet. 73rd/ 74th Streets
718-505-2680
daily 10am-10pm

As with Shamiana, this is Indian cuisine at its most caseous. The sweets and the dishes in the back are awash in milk, yogurt, cream, ghee, butter and cheese. You can pick your way through the menu to find vegan dishes, but is it really worth it?

ONENESS FOUNTAIN HEART [v]

Full service
International vegetarian
$400-12.00 (all cards)
No alcohol

157-19 72md Avenue
(Flushing)
718-591-3663
daily 11:30-9pm
W 11:00-9:00

Yet another restaurant that is operated by disciples of Sri Chimnoy. In addition to the -blue facades that all the restaurants share, they also have in common an uncommon devotion to high culinary standards and service. The dishes to try here are the Duck Surprise, which is made with vegetarian mock duck, and the Vegetarian Meatloaf. My personal favorite was Thai Heaven, which consists of spicy tofu skin in a delicate coconut sauce. It's worth taking a cab from Manhattan for this one.

SHAMIANA

Counter service
North, South, & Gujarati
$2.95-5.25 (no cards)
No alcohol

42-47 Main Street
bet. Franklin/ Blossom Streets
718-539-0042
daily 10:30am-9pm

This is Indian food at it most caseous. The dishes are heavily laden with dairy products, and the owner /manager was rude and uncooperative when we asked which dishes were vegan and which were not.

SMILE OF THE BEYOND [v]

Counter service
International vegetarian
$4.00-6.00 (no cards)
No alcohol

86-14 Parsons Boulevard
(Jamaica)
718-739-7453
M-F 7am-4pm
Sa 7am-3pm

Not all restaurants in Queens are run by followers of Sri Chimnoy, it only seems that way. This astoundingly inexpensive luncheonette serves delicious veggie burgers, and generous salads that would cost the earth in a Manhattan eatery. All three Chimnoy places are worth the trek from Manhattan. At this place, so economical are the prices that the train fare will probably end up costing more than the meal!

THERESA'S VEGETARIAN CREATION [v]

Buffet./counter service
International, American
$3.00-6.00 (all cards)
No alcohol

217-13 Jamaica Avenue
bet. 217th/ 218th Streets
718-464-7100
M-Th 7am-8pm
F 7am-5pm

A devout 7th-Day Adventist, Theresa seemed to bristle when we asked her if her food was "Ital." She grew up in the Virgin Islands and has arrived at her vegetarianism via the teachings of Sister Ellen White and Dr. John Harvey Kellogg. Nonetheless, her mostly vegan cuisine can stand comparison with the best Ital chefs in Harlem and Brooklyn. We especially savored the Sweet 'N' Sour Tofu, Vegetarian Soy Chunks, and the Chick-Pea Balls. Her repertoire of tasty vegan dishes is vast, and the menu changes daily. It's best to arrive early for lunch and early for dinner because her delectable dishes are snapped up quickly.

NOW YOU CAN ALSO VEG OUT IN CHICAGO!

OVER 100 PAGES

Marla's Vegan Guide to Chicago & the Universe — Marla Rose

Restaurants, Shopping, Veg Groups, Rants and More

FROM THE CREATORS OF VEGAN STREET
www.veganstreet.com

• drink well • be well •

liquiteria

- organic juices
- norwalk-cold pressed bottled juices
- raw-live-smoothies
- liquid-meals
- hot & cold tonics
- nyc "best" oatmeal with 10 toppings

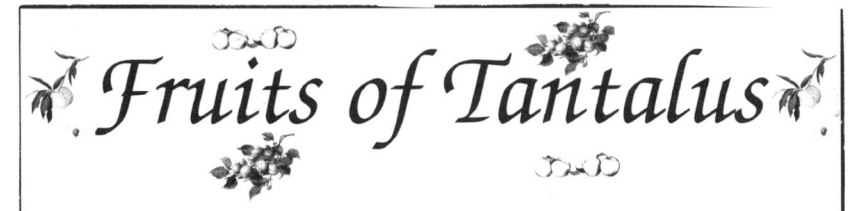

Doug Green's Liquiteria
170 2nd Ave
NYC 10003
212-358-0300

Fruits of Tantalus

A History of Vegan Rawfoodism and the Origins of Cooking

by
Rynn Berry

To be published by Pythagorean Publishers in FALL 2006

PYTHAGOREAN PUBLISHERS
P.O. Box 8174, JAF Station, New York, NY 10116 Tel./Fax: 718-622-8002

Rynn Berry
Food for the Gods
Vegetarianism & the World's Religions
384 pages 0-9626169-2-3 $19.95 paperback

"*Food for the Gods* is eloquently philosophical; it is eavesdropping on the erudite."—**Dr. Kristin Aronson**, Professor of Philosophy, Western Connecticut University

"Rynn Berry has created a memorable feast for mind, body, and soul. *Food for the Gods* makes a tasty and terrific gift for the cook who has everything, including a lively curiosity and an adventurous culinary spirit."—**Lorna Sass**, author of *Lorna Sass' Complete Vegetarian Kitchen*

"The aptly named Rynn Berry has become the official vegan ambassador. His books treat vegetarianism not merely as a cult but as a culture. For Berry, the act of eating is not just a matter of sustenance, it's also a novel and even a spiritual act. His latest, *Food for the Gods*, is a fascinating investigation into the world's great religions. Berry provides illuminating essays on vegetarianism in Jainism, Hinduism, Buddhism, Sufism, and other non-Western religions, as well as Christianity and Judaism. He interviews religious thinkers who are also vegetarians, and he supplies recipes for dishes that have come from these different cultures. The result is a banquet for the taste buds of the mind."—**Jack Kroll**, Senior Editor *Newsweek*

Rynn Berry is the historical advisor to the North American Vegetarian Society and the author of *The New Vegetarians* and *Famous Vegetarians and Their Favorite Recipes*, a biographical history of vegetarianism that ranges from Pythagoras and the Buddha through to Isaac Bashevis Singer and the Beatles. He lives in Brooklyn.

Also by Rynn Berry:
Famous Vegetarians and Their Favorite Recipes: Lives and Lore from the Buddha to the Beatles
The New Vegetarians

TOP TEN JUICE BARS

Although they don't yet outnumber the alcohol bars, or the coffee bars, juice bars are starting to crop up all over town. Unhappily, many of them--like Gray's Papaya--serve meat along with their smoothies and juices. [Recently, we had to drop Juice Generation for serving Chicken Sandwiches.] So we picked places that serve only vegan dishes to go with their drinks. Not so long ago, New Yorkers used to start the day with a shot of bourbon or a mug of java; now, as like as not, they'll get their hearts started with a shot of "green plasma"--wheat grass juice, brimming with enzymes, anti-oxidants, chlorophyll, and phytonutrients.

DOUG GREEN'S LIQUITERIA [v]

170 2nd Avenue
bet. 11th and 12th Streets
daily 8am-10:30pm

The standard by which all others are measured. The best smoothies in the universe! This is the only juice bar in the city that uses 100% organic, fresh fruits and juices.

Doug's criteria for hygiene and service are exacting. Working surfaces and equipment are constantly being scrubbed with an unsleeping vigilance. Well-mannered, eager-to-please, and efficient, his staff clearly love their work as most have been in Doug's employ for six years!

His is the only juice bar in the city that uses a Norwalk hydraulic press. (Up to five times more of the enzymes, minerals and vitamins are expressed in the juices by this method than by any other.) For a bracing sandwich, try Doug's Tempeh Bacon Lettuce and Tomato. For a Smoothie, try the Papaya Paradise (papaya peaches, banana, apple cider, vanilla soy milk, shredded coconut) They're a ticket to esophageal paradise.

BLUE GREEN [ve]
(3 locations)

248 Mott Street
bet. Houston/ Prince
203 East 74th Street
bet. Second/ Third Avenues
25 Jay Street (Dumbo)
bet. John/ Plymouth Streets

The great thing about Blue Green is that they and JivamukTea are the only juice bars in NYC that are 100% vegan. Practically every other juice bar in the city laces its smoothies and juices with bee pollen or whey (a derivative of cow's milk). For instance, Jamba Juice adds it to its smoothies willy-nilly. You actually have to demand of the Jamba Juicers that they hold the "enlightened base"--a witch's brew of additives of which the principal ingredient is whey. On the other hand, Blue Green offers "enhancers" that are cruelty-free, and healthful--such as Goji Berries, Acai and Hemp Protein. We chugalugged their blended smoothies such as No 11 (cacao, black cherry, banana and coconut water). or No. 12 (pear, almond milk cinnamon, and hemp protein).

Instead of the meat sandwiches that are served at juice bars like Elixir and Juice Generation, et al.--Blue Green serves delicious vegan rawfood delectables like their Spicy Mango Spring Roll (crispy vegetables, young coconut, green papaya, and fresh herbs).

JIVAMUKTEA[ve]

841 Broadway
bet. 13th/ 14th Streets
daily 10am -9pm

This and Blue Green are the only two 100% vegan juice bars in the city. In fact their menu says "100% vegan, organic when humanly possible." The JivamukTea juice bar is actually part of the JivamukTea Cafe in the Jivamukti Yoga Center. To eliminate the remorseless buzz of the juicers and blenders, the juices and smoothies are concocted in a glass-enclosed sound-proof room. Fittingly enough, the smoothies are named after each of the chakras. We are partial to "Third Eye" (mango with young coconut and vanilla).We also relished "Heart" (banana-chai with almond milk). Thanks to the owners of JivamukTea, Sharon Gannon and David Life, who are ethical vegans, no animal-derived supplements are used to boost the smoothies. Instead they offer such enhancers as Acai (from the Brazilian rain forest), Peruvian Maca and Coconut Butter. To help you focus on your mundane activities after your yoga session, you might want to follow your smoothie with a Reality Sandwich. Our favorite is the Creator (soy bacon, baby bibb lettuce, heirloom tomato and chipotle mayo on wheat).

JUBB'S LONGEVITY [v]

508 East 12th Street
bet. Avenues A/ B
daily 10am-9pm

Dr. David Jubb is as much an alchemist with juices and smoothies as he is with food. Try his incomparable Amazon fruit smoothies such as the Acai, or the Passion Fruit. Or have his Mixed Berry Smoothie. Have a raw vegan Burger Deluxe for David's unfired vegan version of the all American combo of Burger 'n' Shake.

RAW SOUL[v]

348 West 145th Street
bet. St. Nicholas/ Edgecomb
daily 9:am-9pm

This rawfood delicatessen-cum-juice bar offers a range of juices and juice combinations along with salads and some tasty raw fruit pies. Try Island Spice (pineapple, papaya, mango, ginger root), or Berry, Berry, Berry Good (strawberry, blueberry and raspberry).It and some of the daily specials like the Personal Pizza, are indeed Berry, Berry, Berry good!

CAFE KAI [v]

151 Smith Street (Brooklyn)
bet. Bergen/ Wycoff Streets

Lisa, the proprietor, makes smoothies and juice combos using exotic rain forest fruits. The quality of the food served here, which is 99% organic and vegan, is as sublime as her smoothies.

JUS [v]

16th Street
at Union Square West,
daily 8am-8pm

Joao, the Brazilian man who runs this stand, concocts delicious smoothies and fruit tonics. His best-selling fruit tonic is an apple-cantaloupe, pineapple combo; and his best-selling smoothie is mango, strawberry and pineapple. It's our favorite as well.

GREENER PASTURES [ve]   Union Square Greenmarket
                                             16th St. / Union Square West
                                             M,W, F, Sa 8am-7pm
On Mondays, Wednesdays, Fridays and Saturdays of every week, Stewart, the proprietor, serves up wheat grass juice and effervescent good humor to the patrons who mob his stand. They swear he has the sweetest grass in the city. A one ounce shot is $2.00 a double shot is $3.50. Stewart also sells flats of Wheat Grass as well as succulent salad greens.

UPTOWN JUICE BAR [ve]   54 West 125th Street
                                             daily 8am-10pm
They offer a wide array of juices and juice combinations that are designed to cure everything from asthma to impotence. The fruit smoothies are delicious, and the Caribbean style vegan food is first rate.

OUTDOOR JUICE STAND [ve]   Corner Newkirk
                                             (Brooklyn)
                                             at Nostrand Avenues,
                                             11am-6pm
365 days a year, the members of this West Indian family run an outdoor juice stand where they make fresh coconut juice and sugar cane juice. After you sip the coconut water from the coconut, an obliging young man will hack it open with a machete, and you can scrape out the tender meat with a scoop fashioned from the coconut shell. The canes and coconuts are imported from Florida.

Exotic Superfoods

THE ONLY 100% RAW FOOD STORE IN QUEENS!

- Juices
- Smoothies
- Salad bar
- Raw foods
- Supplements
- Snacks
- Dried fruits
- Nuts & seeds

All made with organic ingredients.
Serving breakfast, lunch and dinner daily.

Tel: 718-353-4807   185-02 Horace Harding Expy, Fresh Meadows, NY
                     Exit 25 off the LIE. East bound service road.

FOOD SHOPPING

It's possible to eat cheaply in New York. It's also possible to spend your life savings on a single meal (though much easier for meat-eaters than for vegans!). This applies to restaurants as well as to shops, which range from the most luxurious importers to inexpensive, dependable local farm products. Below are some notable places that won't break your budget; for obvious reasons, this is not a comprehensive list. Individual addresses are listed on the following page.

SUPERMARKETS

The largest stores carry health food items, soy milk, and the like, but their prices are not usually any lower than large health food shops for these goods. The New York chains, listed in roughly ascending order of price (quality is quite similar):
Associated, Sloan's, Gristede's, Met Food, D'Agostino, Food Emporium, WholeFoods.

PRODUCE

There are greenmarkets, also called farmer's markets, on certain days in public squares, where producers drive truckloads of fresh and often organic fruits and vegetables into the city from their farms in upstate New York, Pennsylvania, and New Jersey. The prices and quality can't be beat, and there's a festive atmosphere to these events. Of course, you'll find only what's in season, so there are slim pickings during the cold winter months. Union Square is the largest of these, and it boasts a vegan bakery stall called Body & Soul with great treats both sweet and savory.

The next choice for organic produce is shopping at a large health food store like Wholesome Market, Integral Yoga or Commodities. Prices are a bit higher, but the quality is excellent.

For non-organic produce, the Asian shops along Canal Street in Chinatown and on First Avenue around 7th Street in the East Village have the lowest prices. Otherwise, supermarkets and the 24-hour groceries that line many New York streets are fairly reliable.

BULK GOODS, SPICES, ETC.

The larger health food shops all have a section where you can buy grains, beans, nuts, dried fruit, flour and snacks in bulk, most of it organic. For non-organic bulk goods and wonderful spices at low prices, try the Indian shops around Lexington and 28th Street or First Avenue and 6th Street.

FAVORITE SHOPS

HARLEM

FAIRWAY FRUITS & VEGETABLES
Huge produce and natural food store.

2328 Twelfth Avenue
at West 132nd Street

7 GRAINS HEALTH FOODS
Health food shop.

2259 Seventh Avenue
at 133rd Street

UPPER WEST SIDE

CREATIVE
Health food shop.

2805 Broadway
bet. 108th/109th Streets

GARY NULL'S UPTOWN WHOLEFOODS

2307 Broadway
at West 89th Street

Health food grocery with bustling juice bar and kosher vegetarian salad bar.

HEALTH NUTS
Health food shop with juice bar.

2611 Broadway
at West 99th Street

OLIVIERS & CO
Olive oil shop.'

198 Columbus Avenue
at 69th Street

WHOLEFOODS MARKET
Organic supermarket.

10 Columbus Circle
at 60th Street

UPPER EAST SIDE

HEALTH NUTS
Health food shop with juice bar.

1208 Second Avenue
bet. 63rd/64th Streets

MATTER OF HEALTH

1478 First Avenue

Health food shop with juice bar.   at 77th Street

NATURAL FRONTIER   1424 Third Avenue
Organic grocery with emphasis on vegetarian and vegan.   at 81st Street

MIDTOWN WEST

HEALTHY CHELSEA   248 West 23rd Street
Health food shop with juice bar.   bet. Seventh/Eighth Avenues

NICE N' NATURAL   673 Ninth Avenue
Health food shop with juice bar.   bet. 46th / 47th Streets

ORGANIC MARKET   229 Seventh Avenue
Health food shop.   bet. 23rd/24th Streets

SIVANANDA YOGA VEDANTA CENTER   243 West 24th Street
Exercise, breathing, relaxation, diet, and mediation   bet. 7th/8th Avenues

WESTERLY NATURAL MARKET
Well stocked organic grocery.   911 Eighth Avenue
     at 54th Street

WHOLEFOODS MARKET   250 Seventh Avenue
Organic supermarket.   at 24th Street

MIDTOWN EAST

BETH'S FARM KITCHEN   Union Square Greenmarket
Jams, jellies and pickled vegetables F, Sa year-round.   bet. 17th St / Union Sq. West

BODY & SOUL   Union Square Greenmarket
All-vegan baked goods stand. M F year-round.   bet. 17th St / Union Sq. West

FANTASY FRUIT FARM   Union Square Greenmarket
Blueberries, strawberries, raspberries, seedless grapes   bet. 17th St. / Union Sq. West
Saturdays, June-Nov.

FOODS OF INDIA   121 Lexington Avenue
Another Indian grocery.   bet. 29th/30th Streets

HEALTH NUTS   835 2nd Avenue
Well-provisioned health food store.   bet. 44th/ 45th Streets

KALUSTYAN 123 Lexington Avenue
bet. 28th / 29th Streets
Well-stocked Indian Grocery. They feature bulk items such as raw pistachio nuts and sun-dried strawberries.

KEITH'S FARM Union Square Greenmarket
Heirloom herbs, garlics and greens, We Sa, Ju -Nov. bet. 17th St. / Union Sq. West

LOCUST GROVE FRUIT FARM Union Square Greenmarket
A cornucopia of delicious fruit, W, Sa year-round. bet. 17th St. / Union Sq. West

OLIVIERS & CO Grand Central Terminal
Olive oil merchants near Track 17
This store specializes in premium olive oils from all the Mediterranean countries plus Uruguay. They also sell a highly addictive sun-dried tomato powder for sprinkling on salads and suchlike vegan fare.

PHILLIPS FARMS Union Square Greenmarket
bet. 17th/ Union Sq. West
Peaches, Raspberries, Blueberries and Blackberries. March-December, M, Sa 8am-6pm.

RICK'S PICKS Union Square Greenmarket
bet. 17th/ Union Sq. West
Rick, an Andover and Yale alum, quit his job as PBS producer to become a picklemeister. Favorite pickle is Wasabean (green beans and wasabi). Wednesdays sunrise to sunset, year round.

TRADER JOE'S 142 East 14th Street
at Union Sq. East
An offbeat supermarket, Joe's is famous for its unusual and inexpensive products, like wild blueberry juice, dark chocolate-covered espresso beans, and, our favorite, chili-spiced dried mango slices.

WINDFALL FARM Union Square Greenmarket
Wide range of organic greens, We, Sa year round bet. 17th St. / Union Sq. West

GREENWICH VILLAGE

INTEGRAL YOGA NATURAL FOODS 229 West 13th Street
Health food shop bet. Seventh/Eighth Avenues
Good quality and price on organics and bulk goods, plus hot and cold buffet. Some raw food dishes. Very popular.

LIFETHYME 410 Sixth Avenue
at Eighth Street
One-stop shopping for large selection of exclusively organic produce, bulk goods, vitamins, herbal nostrums, and cruelty-free cosmetics. Amazing salad bar and delicious vegetarian food to go. Their vegan bakery turns out scrumptious pastries and prides itself on not using milk eggs or cheese in any of their cakes cookies or pies. They have a spiffy juice bar, and a good selection of

books on nutrition and healing. Recently, they've added a living foods section with delicious raw pies, cakes and entrees.

OLIVIERS & CO   249 Bleecker Street
Olive oil merchants.   bet. 7th / 6th Avenues

ORGANIC MARKET   250 Mercer Street
Large health food shop with bulk section and juice bar.   bet. 3rd/4th Streets

STELLA McCARTNEY   429 West 14th Street
     bet. 9th/ 10th Avenues
The scion of Sir Paul sells vegan shoes and cruelty-free clothing of her own design.

EAST VILLAGE

ANGELICA'S   147 First Avenue
Herbs   at 9th Street
One of the largest selections of herbs, both culinary and medicinal, expensive organic produce.

COMMODITIES EAST   165 First Avenue
     at 10th Street
Health food shop with good quality and prices on organic produce and bulk goods.

4TH STREET FOOD COOP   58 East Fourth Street
     bet. Bowery and Second
All produce from leafy greens to tubers is organic, and the granola, grains, nuts and other bulk times are mostly so. Non-members are welcome.

HIGH VIBE HEALTH & HEALING   138 East Third Street (rear)
     bet. 1st / A Avenues
Raw food nutritional counseling, fasting supervision, classes in rawfood preparation, health care products, books and appurtenances. Try the raw cured olives, and a tasty range of raw snack foods..

INDIA SPICE HOUSE   99 First Avenue
Indian grocery, 24 hours   at 6th Street
Smaller than the Lexington stores, and the foodstuffs don't move so quickly, but still good—especially if you need some fenugreek or asafoetida in the middle of the night. 400 kinds of beer.

JUBB'S LONGEVITY   508 E. 12th Street
     bet. Avenues A / B
Living foods patisserie, life food preparation classes, and a range of super foods and cosmetic products that purport to promote longevity.Try Jubb's Body Ice; and Essential Oils.

JIVAMUKTI YOGA CENTER   841 Broadway
bet. 13th/ 14th Streets
Yoga Center and emporium that sells yoga paraphernalia, eco-friendly clothing, books. It also features a new vegan cafe -cum-juice bar called JivamukTea, Try the Raw Lasagna, the Creator BLT, and chef Matthew Kenney's delicious raw desserts.

LIVE LIVE   261 East 10th Street
bet. 1st Avenue / Avenue A
Raw foods boutique, featuring, a wide selection of books, super foods, snacks, potions, energizers and rejuvenatives. Also on sale are dehydrators, juicers and other accouterments of the raw food lifestyle.

STONEHOUSE OLIVE OIL   273 East 10th Street
bet. 1st Avenue / Avenue A
A store dedicated entirely to olive oil, this is. Not just any olive oil, but a premium California olive oil that stands comparison with the best European olive oils. Our favorites are the citrus oils-- Persian Lime, Lisbon Lemon, Blood Orange. The fruits are pressed with the olives at the first pressing, so the olive oil is deeply infused with their flavors. Stonehouse also sells a balsamic vinegar.

SOHO

BABY CAKES   240 Broome Street
Vegan baked goods.   bet. Orchard/ Ludlow Streets

EARTH MATTERS   177 Ludlow Street
Organic market with salad bar   bet. Stanton/ Houston

GUSS'S LOWER EAST SIDE PICKLES   85-87 Orchard Street
bet. Broome/ Grand
Pickled tomatoes, artichoke hearts as well the old standbys. This shop and its owner starred in the motion picture Crossing Delancey Street.

MAY WAH HEALTHY VEG. FOOD   213 Hester Street
bet. Centre / Baxter
Chinese Vegetarian grocery store. Well-stocked with mock meats such as mock shrimp, mock duck, mock squid, etc.

MOO SHOES   152 Allen Street
bet. Stanton/ Rivington
The best selection of cruelty-free shoes and accessories in the country.

ORGANIC AVENUE   01 Stanton Street
bet. Orchard/ Ludlow
Hemp and organic clothing, organic lifestyle products, fresh, raw and organic produce collective.

VEGECYBER 　　　　　　　　　　　　210 Center Street
　　　　　　　　　　　　　　　　　　　bet. Grand / Canal
All vegetarian grocery store with on-line catalogue. See http:// www. vegecyber.com/

BELOW CANAL STREET

BELL BATES 　　　　　　　　　　　97 Reade Street
Large Health Food Grocery Store 　　　bet. W.Bway / Church

COMMODITIES NATURAL FOODS MARKET 　117 Hudson Street
Vast health food shop with good bulk prices.　 at North Moore Street

BROOKLYN

BACK TO THE LAND 　　　　　　　142 Seventh Avenue
　　　　　　　　　　　　　　　　　　　bet. Carroll Street/Garfield Place
Organically grown produce as well as grains, nuts and dried fruits are on offer. A wide range of books, magazines and tapes are for sale. There is a section for homeopathic remedies. And a well-stocked macro-biotic section.

DOWNTOWN NATURAL MARKET 　　51 Willoughby Street
Organic produce, Juice and Salad bars.　 off Jay Street

FAIRWAY 　　　　　　　　　　　　480-500 Van Brunt Street
The Manhattan food bazaar has come to Brooklyn.　 Red Hook

FORCES OF NATURE 　　　　　　　1688 Sheepshead Bay Road
Organic Groceries, homeopathic remedies, books and music.

FLATBUSH FOOD COOP 　　　　　1318 Corydon Road
　　　　　　　　　　　　　　　　　　　bet.Rugby and Argyle Rds.
Fresh organic produce. Earth-friendly household products. Open to non-members

GOVINDA ORGANIC MARKET 　　387 Atlantic Avenue
　　　　　　　　　　　　　　　　　　　bet. Hoyt/ Bond Streets
Orlando, the manager, who converted Westerly's from pharmacy to health food store, now has his own well-stocked health food market.

LIVING WELL NATURAL FOODS 　382 Seventh Avenue
Health food shop.　　　　　　　　　　at 12th Street

PARK SLOPE FOOD COOP
Members only organic market
Members pay 20% above cost. Closed to Non-members.

782 Union Street
bet. 6th & 7th Avenues

PERELANDRA NATURAL FOOD CENTER
Largest health food store in Brooklyn. Excellent juice bar and book section.

175 Ramsen Street
at Court Street

THE GARDEN
Well-stocked health food shop.

921 Manhattan Avenue
at Kent Street (Willaimsburg)

QUEENS

LINDA'S NATURAL MARKET
Organic produce, vegetarian deli and juice bar.

81-22 Lefferts Boulevard
(Kew Gardens)

NEIL'S NATURAL MARKET

46-10 Hollis Court Avneue
(Flushing)

Organic produce, vitamins, rawfooods, herbs, homeopathy, cruelty-free body care products, and bulk items.

QUANTUM LEAP NATURAL FOOD MKT.
Organic produce, vitamins and supplements

65-60m Fresh Meadows Lane
(Fresh Meadows)

QUEENS HEALTH EMPORIUM
Macrobiotic products, organic produce, juice bar.

159-01 Horace Harding Expy.
(Flushing Meadows).

THE BRONX

GOOD 'N' NATURAL
Exceptionally well stocked Health Food Store

2173 White Plains Road
(bet. Pelham Pkwy/Lydig Ave)

One other place worth knowing about: **Bruno Ravioli** sells fresh and frozen pasta and offers a few amazing varieties of vegan ravioli to take home, like Shiitake Mushroom, Pumpkin, and Florentine (spinach and carrots). There are three stores: 235 East 22nd Street, 2204 Broadway, 1093 Lexington Avenue, and 249 Eighth Avenue.

GREENMARKETS
(Farmer's Markets)

Location	Day of the week	When
Bowling Green (Broadway & Battery Pl)	Tuesday Thursday	Year Round
South Street Seaport (Fulton, Water / Pearl)	Tuesday	Jun-Nov
Tribeca (Broadway & Duane)	Saturday	Year Round
Tompkiins Square (East 7th St./ Ave. A)	Sunday	Year Round
St. Mark's Church (10th Street / Second Ave.)	Tuesday	June-Nov
Abingdon Square (West 12th / Hudson Sts.)	Saturday	June-Nov
Union Square (largest in NYC) (17th St. / Broadway)	Mon,Wed Friday & Saturday	Year Round Year Round
Dag Hammarskjold (East 47th St. / 2nd Ave)	Wednesday Saturday	Year Round Year Round
Balsley Park (W. 57th St. / 9th Ave)	Wednesdy & Saturday	Mid-June-Nov
IS 44 (77th St. & Columbus Ave.)	Sunday	Year Round
West 97th Street (Bet Amsterdam / Columbus Ave.)	8am-3pm Friday	June-Dec
Columbia (116th St. / Bway)	Thursday	June-Nov
Harlem (125th St / Adam Clayton Powell)	Tuesday Tuesday	July-Oct July-Oct
West 175th Street	Thursday	June-Dec

(Broadway)

BRONX

Poe Park (Grand Conc. / 192nd St.)	Tuesday	July-Oct.
Lincoln Hospital (148th St / Morris Ave)	Tu / Fr	July-Nov

QUEENS

Jackson Hts-Traverse Park (34th Ave bet. 77th /78th Sts.)	Sunday	July-Nov

STATEN ISLAND

St. George (St. Marks / Hyatt Sts.)	Saturday	June-Nov

BROOKLYN

Greenpoint-MCarreen Park (Lorimer St.-Driggs Ave)	Saturday	June-December
Williiamsburg (Havermeyer St./ Bway)	Thursday	July-Oct
Bedford-Stuyvestant	Saturday	July-Oct
Grand Army Plaza (at Prospect Park entrance)	Saturday	Year Round
Borough Hall (Montague Street)	Tuesday Saturday	Year Round Year Round
Windsor Terrace (Prospect Park W. / 15th St.)	Wednesday	May-Nov
Sunset Park (4th Ave bet. 59th / 60th Sts.)	Saturday	July-Nov

Quntessence
the essence of food

Pioneering Gourmet
Raw Cuisine Since 1999
Organic · Vegan · Kosher

263 E 10th St.
1av. & av. A
646-654-1823

raw-q.com

Bonobo's Vegetarian Restaurant and Store

18 East 23rd Street
(Between Park Ave So. & Broadway)

Celebrating Live, Raw and Organic
Fruits * Vegetables * Nuts and Seeds
**Naturally Delicious
& Highly Nutritious**
juices * coconuts * blends * soups
salads * patés * sweets * sorbets
and many more vibrant selections...

eat-in
take-out
delivery
catering

www.BonobosRestaurant.com
212.505.1200

BACK TO THE LAND
— Your Natural Foods Grocery Store —

142 7th Avenue
Brooklyn, New York
11215
between Carroll
Street & Garfield
Place

Open 7 days a week
9 a.m. to 9 p.m
Telephone
718-768-5654

www.BackToTheLandNaturalFoods.com

**36th ANNIVERSARY
1971-2007**

Park Slope
Brooklyn's Landmark
Natural Foods Store.

Jubb's Longevity

508 E12th St (ave A ~ ave B)
212 353 5000

organic

innovative culinary creations
*** lifefood heaven ***

*exotic fruit
smoothies*

*fresh salads
nut cheeses
nori rolls*

*pizza
burgers
lasagne
dessert
cakes
fudge*

brazil nut milk

lifefood for a Sustainble future

free lectures (and tastings!) every tues and thurs at 7pm

RAW FOOD RESOURCES

New York has not only the greatest wealth of vegan and vegetarian restaurants in the world, it also has the greatest wealth of rawfood resources. If you count Jubb's Longevity, and Caravan of Dreams, Bonobos, Green Paradise and Think Liquid, New York City now boasts six raw food restaurants, and a growing number of raw food boutiques like High Vibe and Live Live, where the aspiring rawfooder may obtain nutritional guidance, instruction on raw food preparation, raw food snacks and useful gadgets like Food Processors, Saladacos (spiralizers). dehydrators, et al.

Restaurants

Blue Green
Full raw menu

See restaurant section for
all locations

Bonobos
Full raw menu

18 East 23rd Street
bet. Park Avenue/Broadway

Caravan of Dreams
Partial raw menu

405 East 6th Street
bet. First Avenue / Avenue A

Fruit Salads/ Fruit Shakes
Their fruit salads are the best;; their smothies
 second only to Liquiteria's

Corner 46th Street
at Sixth Avenue

JivamukTea
Vegan cafe with predominately raw menu

841 Broadway, 2nd floor
bet. 13th/ 14th Streets

Jubb's Longevity
Full raw menu

508 East 12th Street
bet. Avenues A/B

Doug Green's **Liquiteria**
Best liquid raw food in town

170 2nd Avenue
bet. 11th/12th

The Plant
Raw menu, organic juices, smoothies

25 Jay Street
at Dumbo in Brooklyn

Pure Food and Wine
The *ne plus ultra* of raw food restaurants

54 Irving Place
bet. 17th/ 18th Streets

Pure Juice and Take Away
The take-out editon of Pure Food and Wine

125 1/2 East 17th Street
bet. 3rd Avenue / Irving Place

Quintessence
Full raw menu

263 East 10th Street
bet 1st Avenue / Avenue A

Raw Soul
Raw menu with juices and smoothies

348 West 145th Street
bet. St. Nicholas/ Edgecombe Avenues

Raw Boutiques

Raw boutiques hold lectures, food prep classes; and sell super foods, raw snacks, books, gadgets, cosmetics, and other adjuncts of the vegan rawfood lifestyle.

BONOBOS REAL FOOD STORE
212-505-1200

18 East 23rd Street
bet. Park Avenue/ Broadway

EAT RAW
866-432-8729

125 2nd Street(Brooklyn)
at Bond Street

HIGH VIBE
212-777-6645

138 East 3rd Street
bet. First / A Avenues

JUBB'S LONGEVITY
212-353-5000

508 East 12th Street
bet. Avenues A/ B

LIVE LIVE
212-505-5504

261 East 10th Street
bet. 1st Avenue /Avenue A

ORGANIC AVENUE
212-334-4593

101 Stanton Street
bet. Orchard/ Ludlow

Rawfood Support Groups

NATURAL HYGIENE
212-956-2031

Mondays 7pm-9pm
416 West 46th Street

ACCENT ON WELLNESS
212 760-5953

Wednesdays 8pm-10pm
528 East 5th Street

Raw Potlucks

MANHATTAN POTLUCK
212-254-9453

First Saturday, Dharma Yoga Center
297 Third Avenue

HALLELUJAH ACRES POTLUCK
212-594-0718

Last Sunday 484 West 43rs Street
Apt. 34k (Rev. Lawrence Rush)

Hands On Raw Food Preparation Classes

JUBB'S LONGEVITY	212-353-5000
ORGANIC AVENUE	212-334-4593
THE PLANT	718-722-7541
QUINTESSENCE	212 501-9700
RAW SOUL	212-491-5859

Raw Foods on the Internet

HIGH VIBE	www. highvibe. com
LIVE FOOD	www. Live-Food.com
NATURE'S FIRST LAW	www. rawfood.com
RAWFOODS NEWS	www. rawfoodsnews.com
HALLELUJAH ACRES	www. hacres.com
FRESH NETWORK	www. fresh-network.com
RAW VEGAN INTERNATIONAL	www. rawvegan.com
RAW NUTRTIONAL COUNSELING,	www. doctorgraham.cc

Raw Resorts

Ann Wigmore Natural Health Institute, PO Box 429, Rincon, PR 00677; (787) 868-6307

The Annapurna Inn & Spa, 538 Adams, Port Townsend, WA 98368; (800) 868-ANNA.

Aris La Tham's House of Life at Resource Gardens, Berryhill Road, Irishtown, Negril, Jamaica; (876)944-8209; Sunfirefood@hotmail.com.

Vegan Living Foods Health Spa-Hippocrates Health Institute, 1441 Palmdale Court West Palm Breach, FL 33411; (407) 471-8876

Vegan Health Spa-The Regency Health Spa, 2000 South Ocean Avenue, Hallandale, FL 33009, (800) 454-0003

Water Fasting Center: True North, 4310 Lichau Road, Penngrove, CA 94951; (707) 792-2325

FAVORITE BOOKSTORES

New York is the national capital of the publishing world, and is full of bookstores of all types—large chains carrying bestsellers, small dusty used bookshops, specialized technical or foreign-language stores. Here are some of our hangouts.

ALABASTER BOOKS	122 Fourth Avenue
Tel. 212- 982-3550	at 12th
BOOKCOURT	363 Court Street
Tel. 718-875-3677	bet. Pacific/Dean
BLUESTOCKINGS	172 Allen St.
Tel. 212-777-6028	bet. Stanton/Rivington Streets
COLISEUM BOOKS	11 West 42nd Street
Tel. 212-840-7955	at Fifth Avenue
CRAWFORD-DOYLE	1082 Madiosn Avenue
Tel. 212-288-6300	at 82nd Street
EAST WEST BOOKS	78 Fifth Avenue
Tel. 212-243-5994	at 13th Street
GOTHAM	16 West 46th Street
Tel. 212-719-4448	bet. Fifth/Sixth Avenues
GRYPHON	233 West 72md Street
Tel. 212-874-1588	at Broadway
KITCHEN ARTS & LETTERS	1435 Lexington
Tel. 212- 876-5550	at 94th Street
LABYRINTH BOOKS	536 West 112th Street
Tel. 212-865-1588	bet. Broadway/Amsterdam Avenue
MERCER STREET BOOKS	206 Mercer Street
Tel. 212-505-8615	at Bleecker
OPEN CENTER BOOKSTORE	83 Spring Street
Tel. 212-219-2527 ext. 108	at Broadway
QUEST BOOKSHOP	240 East 53rd Street
Tel. 212- 758-5521	bet. Second/Third Avenues
SHAKESPEARE & CO	716 Broadway
Tel. 212-529-1330	at Waverly Place
ST. MARK'S BOOKSHOP	31 Third Avenue
Tel. 212-260-0443	at 9th Street
STRAND	828 Broadway
Tel. 212-473-1452	at 12th Street
THREE LIVES & CO	154 West 10th Street
Tel. 212- 741-2069	at Waverly Place
USED BOOK CAFE	120 Crosby Street
Tel. 212-334-3124	at Houston Street

BOOKS BY RYNN BERRY

THE NEW VEGETARIANS

Fourteen famous men and women tell why they have joined over 10,000,000 Americans who have turned to vegetarianism.

"Well-written and fascinating..."
—*M.F.K. Fisher*

"Recommended."—*Library Journal*

"If you"re still eating at occasional hamburger, this fascinating account of 14 famous vegetarians may just turn the tide for you."—*Pacific Sun*

192 pages   **$10.95** *paperback*

FOOD FOR THE GODS
VEGETARIANISM & THE WORLD'S RELIGIONS

"Rynn Berry's widely read book *Famous Vegetarians and Their Favorite Recipes* presented the teachings of the great humanitarians and furnished readers with the means of reproducing their preferred dishes. Two thirds of those chosen belonged to the past. His current study deals exclusively with contemporaries, although with roots in the past. Their 'recipes' have a more spiritualized connotation, as they are not human fare but divine ambrosia. Rynn Berry's present offering is truly Food for the Gods."
—***Clay Lancaster***, *author of The Incredible World's Parliament of Religions.*

374 pages   **$19.95** *paperback*

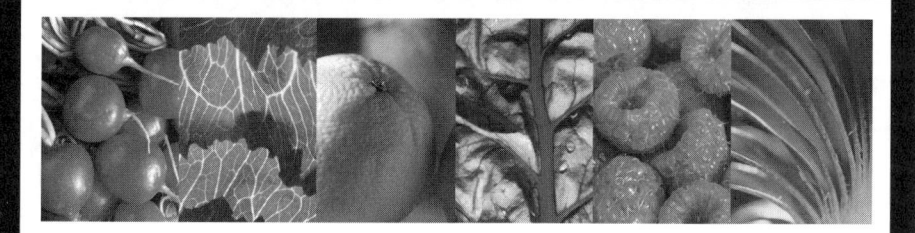

Professional Training Program in Integrative Nutrition & Health Counseling

For 13 years, the Institute for Integrative Nutrition has been delivering leading-edge training in the rapidly-expanding field of holistic nutrition. Our distinctive and comprehensive Professional Training Program teaches a vast array of dietary theories which can be applied to numerous careers and serve to enrich your personal life.

- our world-class curriculum, taught over 10 class weekends in NYC, is designed for busy people who wish to deepen their understanding of nutrition
- study with the nation's foremost pioneers and professionals in nutrition and holistic health, including Dr. Andrew Weil, Deepak Chopra, David Wolfe, and Barry Sears
- discover the foods and the lifestyle that nourish your body and soul
- establish a professional presence through our business support, including marketing materials, a website and business coaching
- upon successful program completion, you will graduate as a Health Counselor, qualifying for national certification as a Holistic Health Practitioner by the American Association of Drugless Practitioners
- choose to receive Continuing Education Units (CEUs) from The Center for Educational Outreach – Teachers College Columbia University

If you are interested in living a long and healthy life, while pursuing your dreams, we are the place for you. Join us in the future of nutrition today.

Call 212.730.5433 extension 1
for more information and to enroll today.

institute for integrative nutrition

GLOSSARY

Baba ganoush	Middle Eastern spread made of eggplant, tahini, chick peas, lemon & garlic.
Bagel	The classic New York bread. Chewy and sprinkled with onion, garlic, or seeds, and shaped like a donut. Eat one and you won't be hungry for hours. Usually vegan; ask about eggs and egg glaze.
Casein	A milk protein that accounts for cheese's ability to melt smoothly. Alas, it is added to nearly all soy cheese, making it unacceptable for vegans.
Chips	To an American, chips are crisps and fries are chips. Get it?
Dim Sum	Asian buffet: a selection of lots of different dumplings, savory cakes and the like.
Eggplant	Aubergine.
Falafel	The vegetarian meatball: a Middle Eastern deep-fried patty of ground chick peas, garlic, and parsley.
Gluten	Chewy bland dough made from wheat flour which absorbs the flavors of the dish or sauce it's cooked in, like tofu. Common meat substitute.
Hummus	Middle Eastern spread made of ground chick peas, tahini, garlic, lemon and olive oil.
Knish	A savory pastry in which a simple thin dough is wrapped around a filling of potato, buckwheat, rice, etc. Usually vegan, but it pays to ask about cheese or butter, and whether the dough is made with egg.
Kosher	Strict dietary guidelines followed by some Jews; they include a prohibition on mixing meat with milk in the same meal or the same kitchen. That means a kosher "dairy" restaurant will have no meat, with lots of options for ovo-lacto vegetarians but nothing for vegans, while a kosher restaurant that serves meat will have no dairy. Likewise, if a processed food is labeled "kosher," it won't contain both animal gelatin and milk powder, for instance.
Macrobiotic	A way of eating from Eastern traditions that seeks to bring foods into balance. Macro restaurants usually serve fish and sometimes eggs, but no dairy; they always have plenty for vegans.

Pico de Gallo	Mexican salsa made from raw onions, tomatoes, garlic, and cilantro.
Pretzel	On the street, these are big warm salty affairs that can stave off hunger in a pinch. They're 100% vegan.
Seitan	Gluten which has been boiled in a ginger-tamari broth.
Soy cheese	Soy milk processed to approximate the consistency and flavor of cheese. It almost always contains casein, a milk protein, so check to make sure it's vegan. (Soymage and Tofutti are typical brands of vegan cheese.)
Squash	A sweet autumn vegetable that comes in many types; pumpkin is one.
Tempeh	Fermented soybeans pressed into cakes, more flavorful than tofu.
Tempura	Vegetables dipped in batter and deep-fried. Ask about eggs in the batter.
Tofu	Tofu is to soy milk as cheese is to cow's milk. Relatively bland, it soaks up the flavors of whatever it's cooked in.
Zucchini	Courgette.

www.vegieworld.com

**Veggie Soul Chicken within a click.
Delivery anywhere in the US.
Vegan. No MSG.
Easy to prepare.
What else do you need?**

**Visit our Retail Store
213 Hester St. NY, NY 10013
212.334.4428**

CRUELTY-FREE SHOES

Until recently, it was scandalous that in New York, one of the world's great pedestrian cities, there were no shops that specialized in selling vegetarian shoes. But now with the advent of shops like Moo Shoes and 99X, you can buy non-leather shoes that are durable, breathable, and good-looking.

MOOSHOES   152 Allen Street
    212 4254-6512
Shoes, belts, and wallets all made by companies that make only leather-free goods.

99X   84 East 10th Street
Has a large vegan/vegetarian shoe section   460-8599

PAYLESS SHOE SOURCE   9 NYC locations; check phone book
Inexpensive, leather-look plastic shoes that last about 6 months.

STELLA McCARTNEY   429 West 14th Street
Non-leather shoes, accessories and clothing.   212-255-1556

WEB SITES

Wear No Evil, www.wearnoevil.net
Hemp Clothing Catalogue, www.hemp-sisters.com
Vegan Essentials, www.VeganEssentials.com
Vegetarian Resource Group, www.vrg.org
Vegetarian Baby and Child Magazine, www.vegetarian baby.com
Vegsource, www.vegsource.com
Veterinarians for Animal Rights, http://avar. org
Friends of Animals, www.friendsofanimals.org
Physicians Committee for Responsible Medicine, www.PCRM.org
Non Dairy, NotMilk.com

MAIL ORDER

PANGEA VEGAN PRODUCTS   283 Lewis Avenue
Rockville, MD 20851
1-800-340-1200
www.veganstore.com
A wide selection of dress shoes, casual shoes, hiking boots, athletic shoes and sandals. They also offer stylish faux leather coats, belts, wallets and bags.

USED RUBBER USA   597 Haight Street
San Francisco, CA 94117
415-626-7855
www.usedrubberusa.com
Wallets, bags, backpacks, dayplanners and address books made from recycled inner tubes.

VEGAN WARES   78 Smith Street
Colingwood, 3066 VIC Australia
03-9417-1200
www. veganwares.com
Shoes manufactured by Vegan Wares may be returned after use for recycling.

HEARTLAND PRODUCTS, LTD.   Box 250
Dakota City, IA 50529
515-332-3087

Vegetarian footwear imported from England.

VEGETARIAN SHOES   12 Gardner Street, Brighton, BN1
British vegetarian shoes.   1UP, England
.0273-691913.

F & O ALTERNATIVE PET PRODUCTS   11252 Fremont Avenue
Vegan pet foods for dogs and cats.   Seattle, WA 98133
877-378-9056
www. vegancats.com

WHY VEGANISM?

Vegetarians avoid meat because of the animal suffering, negative health effects, and environmental damage involved in "eating carcasses," as Leo Tolstoy put it. Vegans carry these reasons to their logical conclusion and avoid using all animal products, to the extent possible.

Cruelty
Milk and eggs are taken from animals kept in horrific conditions on factory farms. Hens are packed into cages so small they would peck each other to death if their beaks hadn't been cut off by a hot knife; these cages are jammed into buildings housing as many as 80,000 birds. After a few exhausting years of laying eggs over conveyor belts with fluorescent lights on 18 hours a day, spent hens are turned into soup. In cows, as in women, there is a connection between lactation and pregnancy: cows only give milk after giving birth. Therefore cows are artificially inseminated every year and their calves are taken away to be slaughtered for pet food or raised for veal in confining crates. Cows are injected with hormones to increase their milk output, tranquilizers to calm them down and antibiotics to keep them from succumbing to the diseases they contract from the unhealthy conditions in which they are kept. After five or six years of this treatment they are slaughtered. (The natural lifespan of a cow is 20 years.)

Health
Eggs are high in cholesterol, which contributes to heart disease, the leading killer in the United States. Milk products such as whole milk, cheese and yogurt are high in cholesterol and saturated fat, which has been linked to heart disease and cancer. Even non-fat milk products can be harmful: recent studies have linked milk consumption to cataracts and a diet high in animal protein to osteoporosis; while the Recommended Dietary Allowance of protein (for men) is 63 grams, vegetarian men consume an average of 103 grams. Intolerance of milk is the most common food allergy, leading to flatulence and respiratory and skin problems. The U.S. Department of Agriculture estimates that 50% of the dairy cattle in the herds along Mexico's northern border—whose milk is sold in the U.S.—are infected with tuberculosis. And everything the cow eats, from antibiotics to pesticide-laden grain, winds up in her milk. The American Medical Association states that a vegan diet provides all required nutrients, including calcium, iron, and vitamin B-12. Olympic gold medalist Carl Lewis is a vegan—need we say more?

Environment
Animals are kept in such concentrations in factory farms or feedlots that tons of their wastes, laden with pesticide and chemical residue, become a hazard. Livestock production accounts for a staggering 50 percent of America's fresh water use. The runoff from cleaning stalls is contaminated and pollutes acquifers and rivers. Eighty percent of the herbicides used in the U.S. are sprayed on soybeans and corn, most of which are fed to livestock. Livestock raising is the primary cause of topsoil erosion in the United States, but that doesn't stop the U.S. government from spending $13 billion on price supports for milk. 64 percent of U.S. agricultural land is used for livestock feed. Shouldn't we eat the grain and leave the cow's secretions for her calf?

FOR MORE INFORMATION

ANIMALS, HEALTH, AND THE ENVIRONMENT

Farm Animal Reform Movement,10101 Ashburton Lane, Bethesda, MD 20817; ☎(888) FARM-USA: www. FARMUSA.org
Farm Sanctuary-Organization for the Rescue and Protection of Farm Animals, PO Box 150, Watkins Glen, NY 14891; ☎(607) 583-2225
United Poultry Concerns, PO Box 150, Machipongo, VA 23405-0150, ☎(757) 678-7875
Society & Animals Forum, PO Box 1297. Washington Grove, MD. 20880-1297. , ☎ (301) 963-4751
Animal People, PO Box 960. Clinton, Washington, 98236-0960, MD. 20880-1297, ☎ (360) 579-2505
People for the Ethical Treatment of Animals, 501 Front Street, Norfolk, VA 23510; ☎(757) 622-PETA
Friends of Animals 1841 Broadway, #812 , New York, NY 10023, ☎(212) 247-8120
Animal Legal Defense Fund, 127 Fourth Street, Petaluma, CA 94952, ☎ (707) 769-7771
North American Vegetarian Society, PO Box 72, Dolgeville, NY 13329, ☎ (518) 568-7970
New York City Vegetarians, ☎(718) 805-4260 Les Judd, or celiaveg@aol.com
The New York Everything Veggie Meetup, www. vegetarian meetup.com/360/events/5132180/
American Vegan Society, 56 Dinshah Lane, PO Box 360, Malaga, NJ 08328, ☎(856) 694-2877
Monthly Magazine Committed to Vegan Activism-Satya, 539 1st Street, Brooklyn, NY 11215, ☎(718) 832-9556
Institute for Integrative Nutrition, 3 East 28th Street, 12th floor, NYC, NY 10016 ☎ (212) 730-5433. Offers natural cooking classes with no animal products.
Institute for Food and Health and The Natural Gourmet School, 48 West 21st St., 2nd Floor,☎ (212) 645-5170. Natural cooking classes and a $20 Friday night vegan feast.
Earth Save New York, PO Box 96, NY, NY 10108, ☎(212) 696-7986
Earth Save Long Island, PO Box 1313, Huntington, NY 11743, ☎(800) 362-3648.

VEGAN DELIGHTS

Vegan Treats-Vegan Cakes and Pies ☎ (484) 239 8726; www. vegantreats.com
Vegethus Restaurante Best Vegan Satvic Homestyle Cuisine in South America, (11) 5539-3635, www. nutriveg.com.br
Vegan Chocolate Decadence, ☎(800) 324-5018
Vegan Dried Fruits-Rainforest Delights, ☎(626) 284-8001
Vegan Soaps, ☎(877) 833-SOAP
Vegan T-Shirts and Accessories-Vegan Street, ☎(773) 252-0026
Vegan Organic Produce Home Delivery Service-Urban Organic, ☎(718) 499-4321
Vegan Organic Cookies and Brownies-Allison's Gourmet, ☎ (800) 361-8292

✂------------✂-----------✂----------✂----

📝 FEEDBACK ✉

Please write to let us know how we can improve the next edition of *The Vegan Guide to New York City*. Tell us about new restaurants, changes, closings, great meals, whatever you like.

_____
_____
_____
_____

Your address: _____
_____
_____
_____

Additional copies.

For additional copies of *The Vegan Guide to New York City*, send $9.95 plus $1.50 postage each to:

Rynn Berry, 159 Eastern Parkway,
Suite 2H, Brooklyn, NY 11238.
tele/fax: (718) 622-8002.
Email: berrynn@att.net.
Web: vegsource.com/berry.

ALSO AVAILABLE: Rynn Berry's other bestselling books:
• *Famous Vegetarians and Their Favorite Recipes* @ $15.95 plus $3.00 postage.
• *Food for the Gods: Vegetarianism and the World's Religions* @ $19.95 plus $3.00 postage.
• *Hitler: Neither Vegetarian Nor Animal Lover* @ $10.95 plus $2.00 postage.
• *The New Vegetarians* @ $10.95 plus $2.00 postage

For copies of:

The Vegan Passport @ $5.00; *Vegetarian London* @ $10.00; *Vegetarian Britain* @ $13.50; *Vegetarian France* @ $12.00; *Vegetarian Europe* @ $13.50; send the designated amount, plus $2.00 postage, to Attention: Freya Dinshah, The American Vegan Society, 56 Dinshah Lane, PO Box 360, Malaga, NJ 08328 USA.

WOODSTOCK
FARM ANIMAL SANCTUARY

Over 100 rescued farm animals

Open April - October

A short trip by car or Trailways bus

845.679.5955

info@WoodstockSanctuary.org

www.WoodstockSanctuary.org

Learn the truth about Hitler's vegetarianism and love for animals with...

HITLER: NEITHER VEGETARIAN NOR ANIMAL LOVER

RYNN BERRY
Brooklyn, New York

With an Introduction by MARTIN ROWE

Written by a master expositor, leading researcher in the field of vegetarian history and author of such vegetarian classics as FAMOUS VEGETARIANS AND THEIR FAVORITE RECIPES, and FOOD FOR THE GODS: VEGETARIANISM AND THE WORLD'S RELIGIONS.

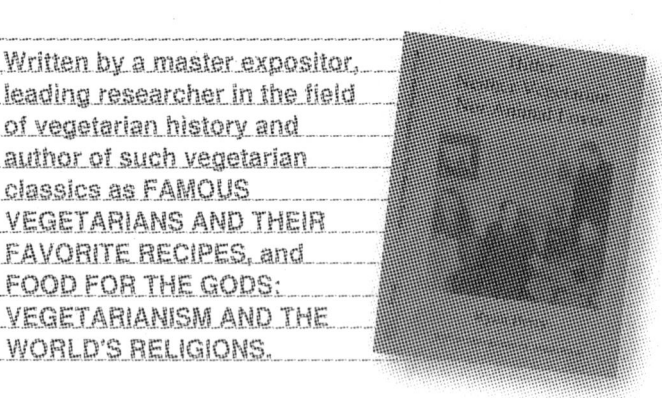

October 2003 / 90 pp. / ISBN: 0-9626169-6-6 / $10.95
Order directly from the publisher (add $2 for shipping):

Pythagorean Publishers
• P.O. Box 8174, JAF Station, New York, NY 10116 •
• 718-622-8002 • berrynn@att.net •

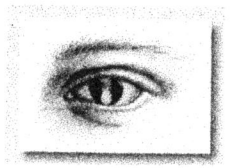

Vegetarian Vision Inc.

Current Events & Activities for 2007
- Summer Cruise in July
- Thanksgiving Dinner in November
- Vegetarian Cooking Classes

Get FREE items as:

-- FREE Car Bumper Sticker
-- FREE Vegan Dinners
(only pay shipping & handling)
-- FREE Vegetarian Vision Information Digest

For these and many more activities, please visit our website at:

http://www.vegetarianvision.org

(201) 792-6335

HANGAWI

a vegetarian shrine
in another place and time

12 East 32nd Street
(between 5th and Madison Ave.)
New York, NY 10016

T. 212. 213. 0077
F. 212. 689. 0780

http://www.hangawirestaurant.com
Email: Info@hangawirestaurant

Original Outspoken Organic

Angelica Kitchen
VEGAN CUISINE

300 East 12th Street
Open 7 days a week
11:30 am - 10:30 pm
ASK ABOUT OUR DAILY SPECIALS

228 - 2909

Franchia

vegetarian cuisine
tea and gift shop
tea workshops
tea parties and events

www.franchia.com
12 Park Avenue
(between 34th and 35th street)
New York, NY 10016
Ph : 212.213.1001
Fax: 212-213-2527

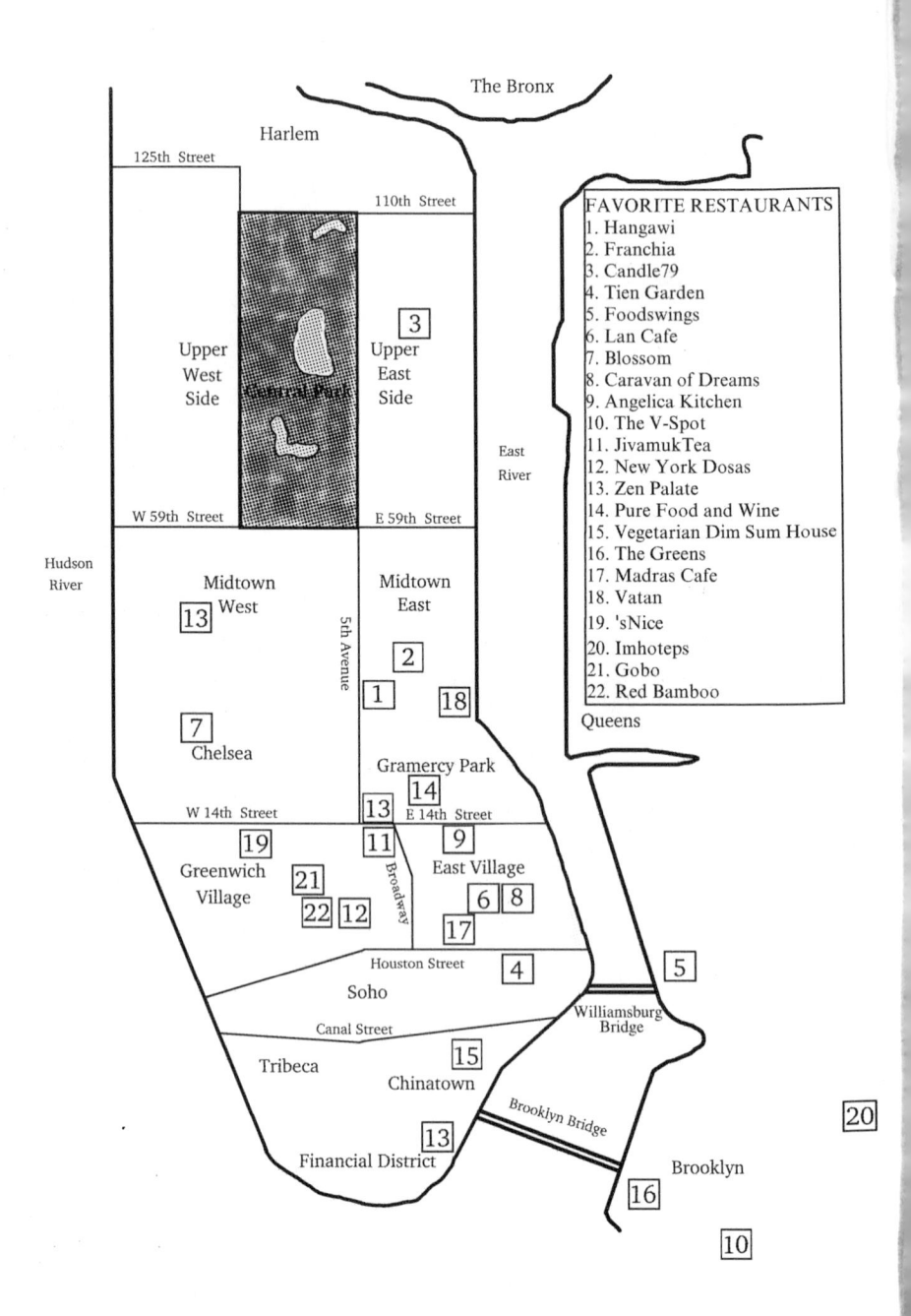

FAVORITE RESTAURANTS
1. Hangawi
2. Franchia
3. Candle79
4. Tien Garden
5. Foodswings
6. Lan Cafe
7. Blossom
8. Caravan of Dreams
9. Angelica Kitchen
10. The V-Spot
11. JivamukTea
12. New York Dosas
13. Zen Palate
14. Pure Food and Wine
15. Vegetarian Dim Sum House
16. The Greens
17. Madras Cafe
18. Vatan
19. 'sNice
20. Imhoteps
21. Gobo
22. Red Bamboo

GO VEGAN

for the animals, the planet, & optimal health

Vegan Lifestyle Coach
Andrew Glick
Certified Holistic Health Counselor
845-679-7979

MEAT FREE ZONE

andy@meatfreezone.org
www.meatfreezone.org

Complimentary Initial Phone Consultation

MAHGO'S
Naturally Wholesome
Pure GREEN MEAL

Freeze-dried organic raw food powder

- 47 different organic raw vegetables
- concentrated micronutrients
- chlorophyll, plant-embryo, etc.
- detoxifier & daily nutritional source

AVAILABLE IN HEALTH FOOD STORES NOW!
www.organicgreenmeal.com
tel: 201-768-1129

NEW YORK OPEN CENTER

Hundreds of exciting:
- talks
- performances
- workshops
- conferences
- professional trainings
- graduate degrees and more!

Visit our bookstore, wellness center & public meditation room

For additional information please call 212-219-2527 x 2 or visit www.opencenter.org

New York Open Center
83 Spring Street
New York, NY 10012

Foodswings

Vegan Fast Food Joint
295 Grand Street Brooklyn, NY
718 388 1919

GUERRILLA VEGAN

www.foodswings.net
www.myspace.com/foodswings

"Some of the best fried chicken I ever ate! And it's not even chicken."
—Sam Champion, Eyewitness News

So this guys asks,
"What's the deal with Wheatgrass?"

So I tell him, drink 1 or 2 ounces a day. It's fresh, sweet and you'll soon learn to love it. But, here's the best part.

In a few days, you'll begin to **feel better... more alive.** Wheatgrass is good for your digestive system, can prevent cancer, diabetes & heart disease, cure constipation, detoxify heavy metals from the bloodstream, cleanse the liver, prevent hair loss and make menopause more manageable. Plus, your poop will smell better.

Not bad for a teeny glass of bright green juice!

~ Harley Matsil, President

More info?, Give me a call!
(800) WHEATGRASS
(that's 800-943-2847)

PERFECT FOODS
America's Premiere Wheatgrass Grower